SAILING *Through* DINNER

I'd like to dedicate this book to my mother, Rita,
who fed a small army of children every day.

ISBN # 0-9638120-0-9
Copyright 1993

Edited by Annice Estes

Published by Three Squares Press
17 Oak Street, Lords Point, Stonington, CT 06378
(203) 535-1151

Design by LaPointe Design
P. O. Box 547, Old Mystic, CT 06372
(203) 536-0879

Printed in U.S.A.

Table of Contents

Welcome!

The Mystic area is rich in history and architecture, warmed by friendly faces, and bursting with sensuous opportunities. You can watch the tides come in and the boats sail by, smell the salt air, hear the buoy bells and fog horns and feel the warm sand between your toes as you stroll the beaches. Minutes away from the shoreline you are confronted with a patchwork of dairy farms, open meadows, and stands of majestic trees defined by stone walls, sparkling brooks, and winding country roads. As if that isn't pleasant enough, at the end of any given day you can experience exquisite dining at some very special places— village cuisine at its finest.

Take this book home with you, put your feet up and close your eyes. Conjure up beautiful images, deliciously vivid aromas, and pleasant memories of your time spent here. If you've never had the pleasure of visiting my home town, read this book as a culinary travel guide and every chapter will welcome you home too.

Enjoy this book by trying these recipes with friends and family. Cooking together is a wonderful way to slow life down just a little and appreciate the basic things we take for granted.

It's in my nature to worry, but I am especially concerned about our inner city children. When they are confronted everyday with random violence and very serious adult choices, the last things they should have to worry about are food and shelter. Those basic necessities should not be options in a country as wealthy as ours. It gives me great pleasure, therefore, to be able to donate the profits from the sale of this book to organizations such as The Children's Soup Kitchen in New Haven who employ unique tactics to break the cycle of poverty—organizations that share a hope of mine that perhaps 10 years from now the children we helped today will have chosen education as their ticket out.

Acknowledgements

The generosity of many people made this book a reality. For individuals to give of themselves and for businesses to donate money, materials, or services meant real sacrifices. Thank you all for your commitment to this project!

Design, Layout, Graphics: Trish Sinsigalli LaPointe

Recipe Testing: Amy Havens, Peg & Bill Twasutyn, Tina Lord, Lynda Galetta, Milt & Phyllis Schumacher, Barbara Sorensen, Joanne & Ron Millovitsch, Mary Terrance, Jane Akins, and Donna Simpson

Wine Recommendations: Gus Holly at Old Mystic Wine Cellar

Writing and Proofreading: Jill Bonner & Dede Wirth

Photography: G. Allan Brown

Pre-production services: J. R. Phil Photographic Lab Services, Pro Color, Blazing Graphics

Paper: RIS Paper Company, Champion International Paper, Butler Paper, Carter Rice Paper Company

Printing: Thames Printing Company, The Harty Press

Binding: Efficiency Mailing and Bindery, Bob Schlump, President

Public Relations: Charly Laura Uman at David Kratz & Company, Inc.

Contributions: Peoples Bank, Chelsea-Groton Savings Bank, Fleet Bank

Special thanks to **Tony Giallombardo** for his efforts in research, recipe-testing, editing, and coordination. Without his help the project would not have gotten off the ground.

Much appreciation also to **Cliff Bentsen and Tara Giallombardo** and many friends for expert taste testing and support in ways too numerous to mention.

Lastly, my compliments to the chefs! This book would still be an idea keeping me awake nights were it not for the cooperation of so many chefs and restaurant owners.

ANTHONY J'S RISTORANTE

Beautiful brick and granite walls greet you as you enter Anthony J's. Constructed in the 1800's and last renovated in 1983, it has the perfect atmosphere for a fine Italian meal. Anthony J's has been cooking to order with only the freshest ingredients since 1985. Be prepared to top your meal off with their special cappuccino and espresso. A full bar is available and brunch is offered every Sunday.

Anthony J's Ristorante
6 Holmes Street
Mystic, CT 06355

Telephone Number: 203-536-0448

Credit Cards Accepted: MasterCard, Visa

Anthony J's Ristorante
Menu

Baked Cherrystones
Tomato and Sausage Soup with Cheddar
Spinach Mozzarella Salad
Chicken Français
Cappuccino Cheesecake

Wine with Appetizer: Italian Gavi
Wine with Entree: French Pouilly-Fumé

The hardest part of this recipe is opening the clams. Try putting them in the freezer for just a few seconds. Sometimes they'll open up just enough to allow your "quahog" knife between the two shells.

Baked Cherrystones A.J.'s
Serves 6

30 cherrystone clams
15 sundried tomatoes, halved
3 tablespoons pesto
1/4 pound sliced provolone cheese,
    quartered

1. Preheat oven to 350 degrees.

2. Wash clams and open as for clams on the half shell.

3. Place 5 clams in each of 6 individual casserole dishes.

4. Place one sundried tomato half on each clam, sprinkle with pesto, and top with provolone to cover.

5. Bake approximately 10 minutes until cheese is melted and clams are warmed through.

6. Serve immediately.

This is a thick and hearty soup that is a substantial prelude to dinner.

Tomato and Sausage Soup with Cheddar
Serves 6 to 8

1/2 pound Italian hot sausage
2 tablespoons olive oil
1 medium Spanish onion, chopped
1 tablespoon garlic, chopped
1 tablespoon flour
1 28-ounce can crushed tomatoes
2 12-ounce cans V-8 juice
1 pinch cinnamon
1 bay leaf
1/2 pound cheddar cheese, shredded

1. Remove casings from sausage.
2. Heat oil in medium saucepan until hot over medium-high heat.
3. Add sausage and onion to oil and cook until onions are translucent and sausage is cooked through.
4. Add garlic and saute for 3 to 4 minutes.
5. Add flour and cook for 2 to 3 minutes.
6. Add tomatoes, V-8 juice, cinnamon, and bay leaf.
7. Reduce heat and simmer for 20 minutes.
8. Ladle into individual bowls and top with cheddar cheese.
9. Serve immediately.

You've probably never had a salad that is so simple to assemble, colorful, and tasty.

Spinach Mozzarella Salad
Serves 6

10 ounces fresh spinach
1 pound mozzarella, sliced
2 large, ripe tomatoes, sliced
6 slices mozzarella, halved
4 tablespoons pesto
1/4 cup extra virgin olive oil

1. Wash and dry spinach; remove stems. Divide onto chilled salad plates.

2. Alternate slices of mozzarella and tomatoes on top of spinach.

3. Mix pesto with olive oil and drizzle over cheese and tomato slices.

The beauty of this lemon-wine sauce is its simplicity.

Chicken Français
Serves 6

6 pieces of boneless chicken
 breast (about 2 pounds)
Flour for dredging
3 eggs, beaten
4 tablespoons butter
Salt and pepper, to taste
Juice of 2 lemons
1 cup dry white wine

1. Remove skin and cartilage from chicken. Pound chicken pieces until very thin.

2. Dip pieces of chicken in flour to coat and then eggs.

3. Melt butter in 2 saute pans over medium-high heat. When foaming stops, add chicken and brown two minutes on each side.

4. Saute for 2 minutes longer. Salt and pepper to taste.

5. Add lemon juice and wine and continue to cook until liquid is reduced by half.

6. Serve with your favorite starch and perhaps al dente broccoli.

The rich coffee flavor of this cheesecake will keep you coming back for more.

Cappuccino Cheesecake
Serves 10 or more

1/3 of a box of graham crackers,
   crushed (1-1/2 cups)
1/4 cup sugar
4 tablespoons melted butter
1 tablespoon instant coffee
1/2 cup boiling water
3 8-ounce packages cream cheese,
   room temperature
1-3/4 cups sugar
3 large eggs
1/2 cup sour cream

1. Preheat oven to 400 degrees.
2. Mix graham cracker crumbs, 1/4 cup sugar, and melted butter until well combined. Press into 10-inch springform pan and bake for 10 minutes. Remove from oven and reduce temperature to 300 degrees.
3. Mix instant coffee into boiling water. Let cool to room temperature.
4. Beat cream cheese at medium speed for 2 minutes and scrape bowl. Lower speed to medium-low and add 1-3/4 cups remaining sugar in a steady stream. Mix until sugar dissolves, about 2 minutes.
5. Add eggs one at a time, mixing well each time.
6. Stop mixer and add sour cream and coffee. Mix on low until just combined.
7. Pour into crust and bake for 90 minutes. Turn oven off and let cheesecake remain inside for 1 hour, to minimize cracking.
8. Chill overnight and serve chilled.

THE BOATYARD CAFE

Overlooking Stonington Harbor, with optional al fresco dining, The Boatyard Cafe offers terrifically imaginative cuisine at reasonable prices. With its friendly atmosphere and dishes that are individually tailored, this restaurant has a personal warmth that really makes you feel like you've come home. The food is exquisite. The talents of co-owner/chefs are many: Deborah Jensen is a culinary arts teacher, author, and winner of the New York Times apple pie contest; Wendy Whiteall is well-versed in Italian cuisine having cooked in Rome for many years. Here they share a delicious, down-to-earth menu with innovative twists. Enjoy!

The Boatyard Cafe
at Dodson's Boatyard
194 Water Street
Stonington, CT 06378

Telephone Number: 203-535-1381

Credit Cards Accepted: None, Cash and Checks Only
Note: There are no alcoholic beverages served,
but you are free to bring your own.

The Boatyard Cafe
Menu

Stuffed Mushrooms
Garden Potato Soup
Dijon Balsamic Vinaigrette
Orange-glazed Roast Pork
Smashed Potatoes
Ratatouille
Apple Cranberry Crunch

Wine with Appetizer: California Sauvignon Blanc
Wine with Entree: French Alsation Riesling

You must always remember that you have options in cooking.
Use this recipe to make stuffed mushrooms 4 different ways!

Stuffed Mushrooms
Serves 4

1 pound mushrooms,
  approximately 12
1 tablespoon butter
1 tablespoon oil
1 small onion, chopped
1 clove garlic, crushed
1/4 cup fresh parsley, chopped
1/3 cup bread crumbs
1/4 cup grated parmesan cheese
1 egg
Options:
  roasted pignoli (pine nuts)
  browned ground beef
  finely shredded crabmeat
  finely chopped, seeded ripe tomatoes

1. Wash mushrooms. Detach and chop mushroom stems.

2. Melt butter in a saute pan and add oil and onion, cooking slowly until translucent. Add garlic and mushroom stems and cook for 2 minutes or so until they start to become soft. Remove from heat.

3. Add parsley, bread crumbs, cheese and an optional item, if desired, and mix well. Add egg and stir quickly to incorporate.

4. Put stuffing into the mushroom caps. This can be done 24 hours in advance, in which case bring back to room temperature before baking in a pre-heated 350 degree oven for 15 to 20 minutes. Serve while hot.

Throw away all your other potato soup recipes. This is all you'll ever need!

Garden Potato Soup
Serves 4-6

2 tablespoons butter
1 large yellow onion, chopped
2 shallots, minced (or 2 leeks or
    1 bunch scallions or all!)
6 cloves garlic, roughly chopped
4 Idaho potatoes, peeled and quartered
Chicken stock or water, about 1 quart
Salt and pepper, to taste
Pinch nutmeg
1 cup milk or cream
Parsley, chopped

1. Melt butter in a soup pot and add all of the onion-type vegetables. Cook very slowly for about 5 minutes until onions start to get translucent. Add garlic for a few minutes. Do not brown. Keep heat low.

2. Add potatoes and mix well. Add stock or water until all vegetables are well covered and bring to a boil. Lower heat to medium and simmer about 20 minutes until potatoes are done.

3. Strain vegetables, saving liquid. Puree vegetables in a blender or food processer.

4. Combine vegetable puree with liquid back in the soup pot. Taste and adjust seasoning with salt, pepper, and nutmeg. Over medium-low heat add milk or cream and heat well without boiling.

5. Serve hot garnished with parsley.

Looking for a great, basic salad dressing? Look no further!

Dijon Balsamic Vinaigrette

2 tablespoons Balsamic vinegar
1 egg yolk
1 tablespoon Dijon mustard
1/2 teaspoon honey
1 teaspoon salt
1/2 teaspoon pepper
1 clove of garlic, minced
1 tablespoon water
3/4 cup olive oil

1. Combine vinegar, egg yolk, mustard, honey, salt, pepper, garlic, and water either by whisking in a bowl or shaking in a jar.
2. Trickle in oil, beating well.
3. Serve with your favorite salad greens.

When you want rave reviews, serve this magnificent roast. Warning: The aroma while roasting may draw unauthorized personnel into the kitchen. Be firm. They must wait for dinner!

Orange-Glazed Roast Pork Loin
Serves 8

3 cloves of garlic, cut in slivers
5-pound boneless pork loin, trimmed and tied
Salt and freshly-ground black pepper
1 tablespoon dried or
  2 tablespoons fresh rosemary, crushed
Approximately 6 ounces orange juice
  concentrate, thawed
Approximately 4 ounces bitter orange marmalade
1 cup navel orange sections
1/2 cup freshly-squeezed orange juice

1. Preheat oven to 325 degrees.

2. Insert garlic slivers in the pork loin and rub with salt, pepper, and crushed rosemary. Put roast in uncovered pan and begin roasting.

3. Estimate your roasting time, using 25 minutes per pound.

4. Half way through your estimated roasting time, baste with some of the undiluted orange juice concentrate.

5. Roast 20 minutes more and then spread the pork loin with the bitter orange marmalade.

6. Roast another 30 minutes and baste with the orange juice and marmalade again.

7. Roast until done and transfer to platter. Skim fat from juices and add orange sections and orange juice. Season to taste and serve with sliced, roasted pork loin.

Want a slightly different twist for an old standby? Here it is,
but remember once again, there are even more options.

Smashed Potatoes
Serves 8

8 Idaho potatoes
2 cups milk
8 tablespoons butter
2 tablespoons horseradish
Salt and freshly-ground pepper,
    to taste

1. Bake potatoes in oven until done, approximately 1 hour at 375 degrees.
2. In a saucepan heat milk and butter together until butter is melted.
3. Cut hot potatoes in half, and using an oven mitt to hold the potato halves, scoop potatoes into a bowl. Add horseradish. Work quickly as all ingredients must be hot or starch in potato will stiffen.
4. Pour hot milk and butter mixture into potatoes and mash with a masher until desired consistency. Do not be alarmed by the amount of liquid. It will all be absorbed by the potatoes.
5. For a different taste, omit horseradish and add 1 sweet potato, or cheddar and parmesan cheese, or sour cream and chives. Potatoes are very versatile.
6. Season with salt and pepper and serve hot with entree.

A recipe this substantial and this tasty could be a meal in itself.

Ratatouille
Serves 6

1 eggplant, peeled
2 zucchini or yellow squash
1 large onion, chopped
1 green pepper
1 red pepper
5 plum tomatoes or 1 18-ounce can
1 large onion, chopped
4 cloves garlic, chopped
2 tablespoons vegetable oil
Oregano
Salt and pepper
Thyme
Rosemary

1. Preheat oven to 350 degrees.
2. Cut all eggplant, zucchini, onion, pepper, and tomatoes into 2-bite sized cubes.
3. Saute onion and garlic in oil in an ovenproof pan until translucent.
4. Add eggplant, zucchini, and peppers, oregano, salt, pepper, thyme, and rosemary to taste. Combine well and cover. Use foil if there is no lid.
5. Bake in oven for approximately 30 minutes or until eggplant pierces easily with a fork. Add tomatoes and roast for 10 minutes more.
6. Serve hot with entree or serve cold as a salad or side dish.

*Because cranberries are a seasonal crop, be sure to keep a bag or two in the freezer
reserved for recipes as good as this one for year-round enjoyment.*

Apple Cranberry Crunch
Serves 8

3 cups McIntosh apples, cored and
   coarsley chopped, leaving peel on
2 cups cranberries
3/4 cup sugar
1-1/2 cup oats (not instant)
3/4 cup almonds, chopped
1/2 cup brown sugar
1/3 cup flour
1/2 cup melted butter

1. Preheat oven to 350 degrees. Grease a round shallow baking dish.
2. Combine apples, cranberries and sugar and place in baking dish.
3. In a bowl, combine oats, almonds, sugar, and flour. Stir in butter until blended.
4. Crumble oat mixture over fruit and press down lightly.
5. Bake 45 minutes.
6. Serve with vanilla ice cream or whipped cream as a dessert. This may also be used as a side dish without ice cream at a turkey dinner.
7. You may substitute 2 large cans drained peaches and 1/2 pint fresh raspberries as an alternative. Another alternative is 6 cups of pitted and chopped plums combined with juice of half a lemon.

RESTAURANT BRAVO BRAVO

Located in the Whaler Inn in downtown Mystic, this eatery is a local treasure. Restaurant Bravo Bravo is a very small restaurant of fourteen tables. There is nothing small, however, about the menu. Served in a casual atmosphere, the contemporary menu with an Italian flavor is sure to please. In fact, the main concern of the staff is satisfying customers with new culinary ideas. Be prepared for a real treat when you dine here—the food is especially delectable and beautifully presented. Next door the Cafe Bravo is run as a separate enterprise with al fresco dining and a different menu.

Restaurant Bravo Bravo
20 East Main Street
Mystic, CT 06355

Telephone Number: 203-536-3228

Credit Cards Accepted:
MasterCard, Visa at restaurant

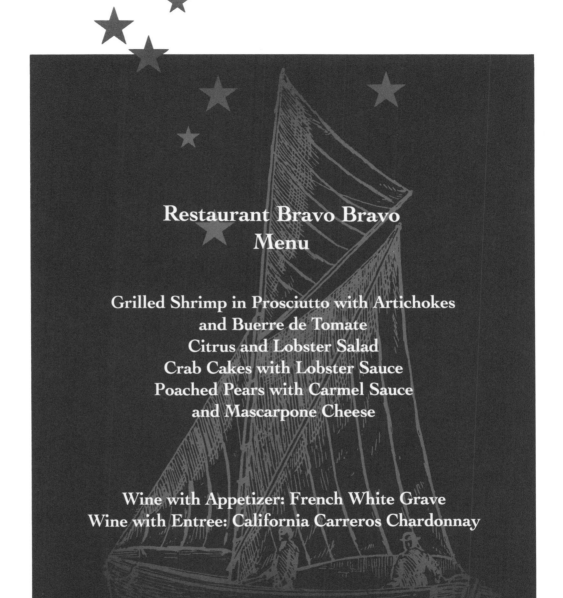

Restaurant Bravo Bravo
Menu

Grilled Shrimp in Prosciutto with Artichokes
and Buerre de Tomate
Citrus and Lobster Salad
Crab Cakes with Lobster Sauce
Poached Pears with Carmel Sauce
and Mascarpone Cheese

Wine with Appetizer: French White Grave
Wine with Entree: California Carreros Chardonnay

Elegant-sounding dishes like this one are not necessarily complicated and are a sure way to make a big impression.

Grilled Shrimp in Prosciutto with Artichokes
Serves 6

1 pound extra large shrimp,
   shelled and deveined
9 or 10 slices prosciutto, cut in half
1 14-ounce can artichoke hearts,
   drained and cut in half
1 cup oil
1 teaspoon black pepper
Juice from 1 lemon
1 red pepper, julienned
1 bunch chives, chopped

1. Cook shrimp on grill for several minutes until just cooked through. Cool.

2. Wrap each shrimp in prosciutto.

3. On 6 skewers alternate the shrimp and artichokes.

4. Combine oil, black pepper, and lemon juice in shallow dish. Marinate skewered shrimp and artichokes in this marinade in refrigerator up to 2 days.

5. Before serving, grill the marinated shrimp kebobs until heated through.

6. Cover the bottom of plate with Buerre de Tomate (recipe follows). Remove the skewer and place shrimp and artichokes on plate. Sprinkle with red peppers and chives and serve immediately.

Use this basic sauce as a backdrop for other dishes too. It's simple, yet effective.

Buerre de Tomate

4 plum tomatoes
2 tablespoons butter
Approximately 2 tablespoons
    chicken or vegetable stock
Salt and pepper, to taste

1. Steam or poach the tomatoes for just a minute or two.

2. Place the tomatoes and butter in blender and puree.

3. Add the chicken stock and process until you get the consistency of a weak milkshake. Add salt and pepper to taste.

4. Keep warm until ready to use or refrigerate and reheat when ready to serve.

When making this recipe, reserve the lobster juice and bodies for the Lobster Sauce recipe.

Citrus and Lobster Salad
Serves 4 to 6

Juice of 1 lemon
1 cup extra virgin olive oil
Salt, to taste
Black pepper, freshly cracked, to taste
4 to 6 cups fresh spinach leaves,
   washed, dried, and stems removed
2 1-pound lobsters, poached,
   cooled and picked
1 leek, cut lengthwise, washed, barely poached,
   cooled, and julienned
1 carrot, peeled, poached, cooled, and julienned
1 orange, peeled and segments separated
1 pink grapefruit, peeled and segments separated

1. Create marinade by combining lemon juice (to taste), olive oil, and salt and pepper.
2. Place spinach in a bowl and toss with just enough of the marinade to lightly coat the spinach and place small mounds on salad plates
3. Place the lobster meat, leeks, carrots, orange and grapefruit sections in the rest of the marinade and toss. Drain off excess marinade.
4. Place the lobster meat in the center of the spinach. Then alternate the orange and grapefruit sections around the lobster meat.
5. Sprinkle the julienned vegetables all over the salad. Garnish with lobster shells.
6. Serve chilled.

Lobster sauce elevates this classic dish to a higher plane!

Crab Cakes with Lobster Sauce
Serves 4 to 6

1/2 onion, diced
1/2 red pepper, diced
1 tablespoon butter
1 pound crab meat
1/2 cup mayonnaise
1 egg
1 teaspoon Worcestershire sauce
1/2 teaspoon Old Bay seasoning
1 tablespoon Dijon mustard
Approximately 20 Ritz crackers,
  crushed
4 or 6 scallions

1. Preheat oven to 425 degrees.
2. Saute onion and red pepper in butter until al dente.
3. In a large mixing bowl, combine all ingredients except crackers and scallions.
4. Slowly add crackers until mixture is stiff. This can be made a day or two ahead of time.
5. Scoop unformed balls of crab mixture (the size of small tennis balls) onto a greased cookie sheet or baking pan. Do not place too closely together.
6. Bake until golden brown, about 10 minutes.
7. Serve in center of plate and pour lobster sauce (recipe follows) over the crab cake.
8. Clean, trim, and cut through scallion greens lengthwise in a cross pattern to form scallion "trees". Soak in ice water until curled and use as garnish. Serve while crab cakes and sauce are hot.

Someday cream sauces this good may be illegal. Enjoy it while you still can.

Lobster Sauce

1 cup lobster juice and stock
   (reserved from lobster salad recipe)
1 cup white wine
3 to 4 mushrooms, sliced
2 to 3 shallots, peeled and minced
1 cup heavy cream
Chives, chopped

1. Place stock, wine, mushrooms, and shallots in small pot and reduce by half over medium-high heat.
2. Add heavy cream to the original depth of liquids in pan.
3. Reduce by half again.
4. Garnish with chives and serve while warm.

Serve this elegant dessert on large dinner plates for dramatic effect. For a lower-calorie alternative, simply serve pears with some of the poaching liquid and a small dollop of whipped cream.

Poached Pears with Carmel Sauce and Mascarpone Cheese
Serves 6

6 pears, left whole
Approximately 1 litre red table wine
1/2 to 1 cup sugar
7 ounces Mascarpone cheese

1. Peel pears, leaving stem on and do not core.
2. In a pan large enough to fit the pears, add enough red wine to cover.
3. Add sugar depending on sweetness desired.
4. Simmer, covered, until pears are soft. This could take 10 minutes to 50 minutes depending on how ripe the pears are. Remove from heat and chill in liquid.
5. Drain pears and reserve liquid. Make 3 parallel cuts partially through pears so they can be fanned out when served. Liquid may be used for poaching another batch of pears if refrigerated.
6. Spoon carmel sauce (recipe follows) onto plates. Top with 1 pear per plate, and add a dollop of cheese on top.

Heating sugar is a little tricky and should be done very carefully. Give it your undivided attention and you should do fine! This is a very simple recipe that yields a delicious, creamy sauce to complement the pears and the whipped cheese.

Carmel Sauce
Makes 1+ cup

1 cup granulated sugar
Water, if needed
3/4 to 1 cup heavy cream

1. Pour sugar into a heavy, shallow, wide saucepan.
2. Melt sugar over medium-low heat, stirring frequently with a long-handled, flat-tipped, wooden spoon. If sugar starts to crystallize on the sides of the pan, brush sides with a small amount of water.
3. When sugar is liquified and slightly browned, take pan off heat and carefully stir in 3/4 cup of heavy cream. Keeping in mind that the carmel will thicken slightly as it cools, add more cream if necessary to thin it out.
4. Serve warm. Refrigerate unused sauce.

CAPTAIN DANIEL PACKER INNE

Captain Daniel Packer purchased the site of this historic inne in 1754, and it has remained in the hands of Packer family descendents ever since then. Weary travelers in the 1700's would stop at the inne and dine on hearty fare while Captain Packer would entertain with thrilling tales of his high-sea adventures. The next morning he would physically transport them across the Mystic River on his rope ferry.

Today the menu will transport food lovers into a state of bliss. The international offerings and traditional dishes are so fresh and so delicious you'll find yourself planning your return trip before you even leave the restaurant! The entire staff at DPI, as locals call it, will be pleased to do whatever they can to make your meal enjoyable, even attending to special dietary needs.

Be sure to visit the lower-level pub where the beer and ale choices and architectural features are equally impressive.

Executive Chef, Michael Stafford, created the following menu using five of his original recipes—the perfect meal for a warm, summer evening.

Captain Daniel Packer Inne
32 Water Street
Mystic, CT 06355

Telephone Number: 536-3555

Credit Cards Accepted: American Express, MasterCard, Visa

Captain Daniel Packer Inne
Menu

Roasted Garlic for Baguettes
Packer Inne Smoked Breast of Chicken with Pasta
Soft-shell Crab and Sweet Red Pepper Soup
Honey Cilantro Grilled Shrimp
with Lemon-lime Buerre Blanc

Carribean-style Rice
Chocolate Hazelnut Toffee Terrine

Wine with Appetizer: Australian Chardonnay
Wine with Entree: California Sauvignon Blanc

When you are seated at the Daniel Packer Inne, warm baguettes, sweet cream butter, and a head of roasted garlic will be brought to your table. The garlic is intended to be slathered onto the baguettes with some of the butter and perhaps a little black pepper. So many people request this recipe it belongs in a cookbook!

Roasted Garlic for Baguettes
Makes 6 heads

6 whole heads of garlic
Approximately 2 cups
 chicken stock or broth
1 to 2 tablespoons virgin olive oil
Salt and Pepper to taste

1. Preheat oven to 400 degrees.
2. Cut the top 3/4 inch from the tops of the heads of garlic.
3. Place the garlic heads (cut side down) in a loaf pan.
4. Add chicken stock to pan until garlic heads are almost submersed and drizzle with olive oil. Sprinkle with salt and pepper.
5. Cover with aluminum foil and bake for 1 hour. Remove the foil and bake an additional 15 minutes or until garlic is nicely browned.
6. Serve hot with bread or baguettes.
7. Reserve unused heads in the refrigerator for other recipes.

You may be tempted to fill up on this appetizer,
but please try to save room for the rest of your meal!

Packer Inne Smoked Breast of Chicken with Pasta
Serves 4

1 Spanish onion, peeled and halved
1 or 2 tablespoons Madeira wine
12 California yellow, sun-dried,
   baby pear tomatoes
White wine
2 tablespoons virgin olive oil
1 head of roasted garlic (see previous recipe)
1 10-ounce smoked breast of chicken,
   cut into strips (grilled may be substituted)
1 small bunch, sweet basil, chopped
Pinch of salt and pepper
1/2 cup dry, white wine
2 tablespoons butter
2 tablespoons Parmesan cheese, freshly grated
4 small servings fresh pasta, cooked al dente
Scallions, thinly-sliced

1. Place the Spanish onion on a piece of aluminum foil and add a splash of Madeira wine. Close foil and grill over hardwood coals until tender. Cut into julienne strips.
2. Soak sun-dried tomatoes in white wine until soft.
3. Heat the olive oil in a medium-sized saute pan until almost smoking, being very careful not to burn.
4. Squeeze the roasted garlic out of the garlic head and combine with the

chicken, basil, Spanish onion, and sun-dried tomatoes. Saute in pan, being careful of spattering. Toss ingredients together in pan for approximately 1-1/2 minutes.

5. Add salt, pepper, wine, and butter. Cook for an additional minute on high heat. Remove from heat and add the Parmesan.

6. Toss mixture together with fresh pasta. Garnish with scallions.

7. Serve while hot.

When soft-shell crabs are in season, this is, without a doubt, DPI's most popular soup. This recipe was created when an overabundance of soft-shell crabs necessitated some quick thinking. The end result speaks for itself. (Editor's Note: This soup is so good you should make it even if soft-shell crabs are not "in season". By substituting shrimp it won't be quite as sweet, but it will still be better than any other soup you've ever tasted!)

Soft-shell Crab and Sweet Red Pepper Soup
Serves 6

1/4 cup olive oil
1/2 cup fresh basil, chopped
1/4 cup fresh oregano, chopped
1 clove garlic, minced
2 large roasted sweet red peppers,
   peeled, seeded and chopped
1/2 teaspoon black pepper, freshly-ground
4 jumbo soft-shell crabs, dressed
   (Ask your fishmonger to show you how.)
1/2 cup medium dry sherry
1/2 cup dry, white wine
2 dashes Worcestershire sauce
1 teaspoon Tamari soy sauce
1 teaspoon Gumbo File spice
   (see mail order sources)
1 teaspoon Old Bay seasoning
1 teaspoon Cajun spice (recipe follows)
2 10-ounce cans chicken broth
2 10-ounce cans beef broth
Zest of 1 lemon
1 cup seasoned bread crumbs

Cajun spice:

Combine equal amounts of ground coriander, cumin, chili powder, cayenne pepper, tumeric, paprika, garlic powder, salt, black pepper, dried basil and dried oregano. Store in an air-tight jar for future use.

1. Heat the olive oil in a large, heavy dutch oven.
2. Lightly saute the basil, oregano, garlic, roasted peppers, and black pepper.
3. Roughly chop the crabs and add to the herb mixture. Add sherry and cook until crabs are cooked through, approximately 5 minutes.
4. Add white wine, Worcestershire sauce, soy, Gumbo File, Old Bay, and Cajun spice and cook over low heat until all the flavors have blended, approximately 10 minutes.
5. Add the chicken and beef broths as well as the lemon zest and bread crumbs. Simmer uncovered for at least one hour, stirring frequently.
6. If necessary, add more bread crumbs as a thickener before serving.
7. Serve hot.

You'll find the subtle tropical taste of these shrimp extremely pleasing.

Honey Cilantro Grilled Shrimp
Serves 4

Marinade:
1/2 cup olive oil
1/2 cup medium dry sherry
1/2 cup clover honey
1 shallot, finely chopped
Juice of 1 lime
1 teaspoon fresh ginger root, minced
1 teaspoon fresh cilantro, chopped
1-1/2 pounds raw jumbo or
    colossal shrimp, shelled and deveined

1. Combine olive oil, sherry, and honey in a shallow dish.
2. Add shallot, lime juice, and ginger root and cilantro.
3. Add shrimp and marinate for at least 24 hours in refrigerator.
4. Grill over hardwood coals until just cooked through.
5. Serve with Lemon-lime Buerre Blanc. (recipe follows.)

This butter sauce is very rich and delicately flavored — the perfect companion to the shrimp.

Lemon-lime Buerre Blanc

Juice and zest of 1 lemon
Juice and zest of 1 lime
1 small shallot, finely chopped
1/2 cup dry white wine
1/4 to 1/3 cup heavy cream
1/2 pound salted whole butter

1. Heat a heavy-bottomed sauce or saute pan and add the lemon juice and zest, lime juice and zest, shallot, and white wine. Using medium-high heat, reduce the liquid by 2/3.
2. Lower heat and add heavy cream, reducing until thick and bubbly.
3. Cut the butter into chunks and slowly add to the mixture until all is incorporated.
4. Set aside and keep warm until the shrimp are ready to serve.

You'll never want plain, white rice again after trying this colorful version.

Carribean-style Rice
Serves 4 to 6

2 cups chicken stock or broth
1 6-ounce package long-grain
  and wild rice mix
2 teaspoons Carribean jerk seasoning
  (see mail order sources)
1 large carrot, julienned
1/2 large sweet red pepper, julienned
1/2 large red onion, julienned
1/4 cup clover honey
2 tablespoons butter
1 scallion, thinly sliced

1. Heat the chicken stock and add the rice and jerk seasoning. Do not use the seasoning packet that comes with the rice. Simmer with cover on over low heat approximately 20 minutes.
2. Add the julienned vegetables, honey, and butter and cook approximately 5 more minutes, or until liquid is absorbed.
3. Garnish with scallions and serve hot with entree.

What finer way to top off an evening than with a piece of this delightful chocolate confection This recipe was developed by pastry chef Bill Hendricks of the Mystic Market. It is our most requested dessert, and once you've tasted it, you'll know why.

Chocolate Hazelnut Toffee Terrine
Serves 8 to 10

Cake:

> 1/2 cup mayonnaise
> 1 cup sugar
> 2 eggs
> 1-1/8 cups all-purpose flour
> 1/4 cup cocoa powder
> 1 teaspoon baking soda
> 1/2 teaspoon baking powder
> 1/2 cup water

1. Preheat oven to 350 degrees.
2. Mix mayonnaise and sugar and add in eggs.
3. Combine flour, cocoa, baking soda and baking powder and add to the egg mixture.
4. Add water in three stages and mix well.
5. Pour batter into a buttered and floured loaf pan 12" x 4" x 3". A standard 9" x 5" x 4" loaf pan may be substituted, but baking time may increase slightly.
6. Bake for 40 minutes or until top springs back when touched.
7. Cool for 10 minutes and remove from pan and slice into 3 equal horizontial layers.

Filling:

12 tablespoons butter

8 ounces semisweet chocolate

5 eggs

1/2 cup confectioners sugar 10x

1/2 cup heavy cream

3/4 cup cocoa powder

1/4 cup English toffee,
  broken into small pieces

1/4 cup white chocolate chips

1/8 cup hazelnuts, chopped

1. Melt butter in double boiler or over low heat.
2. Stir in semisweet chocolate and continue to stir until melted.
3. Separate eggs. Set yolks aside in a large bowl.
4. Whip egg whites with confectioners sugar until stiff.
5. In another bowl whip heavy cream until stiff.
6. Pour butter/chocolate mixture into yolks and mix well. Add cocoa powder and mix until incorporated.
7. Gently fold beaten egg whites and cream into yolk mixture. Then fold in toffee, chips, and hazelnuts.

To assemble terrine:

1. Starting with a layer of cake, alternate cake and 1/2 of filling into loaf pan, ending with a layer of cake.
2. Refrigerate loaf pan for 2 hours.
3. Run warm knife around edges and turn out onto serving platter.

Draw Bridge Inne

Just a few doors down from Mystic's historic draw bridge, Rudy and Marianne Meyer have created a popular local restaurant in the Draw Bridge Inne. Marianne's artwork can be seen on the walls and nightly piano playing will entertain you, but don't let these distract you from the taste of the superb food served here. Rudy trained in Switzerland, Vienna, and Salzburg and worked with world-class chefs for 6 years before striking out on his own. After many years in the Philadelphia area, Rudy came to Mystic 7 years ago. His wealth of experience, personality, and fabulous recipes keep customers coming back again and again.

Draw Bridge Inne
34 West Main Street
Mystic, CT 06355

Telephone: 203-536-9653

Credit Cards Accepted: American Express,
Carte Blanche, Diners Club, Mastercard, Visa

Draw Bridge Inne
Menu

Norwegian Smoked Salmon
Honey Vinaigrette Salad Dressing
Veal Calvados
Glazed Leeks and Rhubarb
Rudy's Apple Strudel

Wine with Appetizer: Brut Champagne
Wine with Entree: German Mosel Kabinett

A colorful, classic appetizer that only requires assembly—perfect for entertaining.

Norwegian Smoked Salmon
Serves 4

Red leaf lettuce
6 ounces Norwegian
   smoked salmon
4 thin slices of red onions,
   separated into rings
4 lemon wedges
4 slices cream cheese, 1/4" thick
3 to 4 tablespoons capers,
   drained
4 slices home-made bread
   or saltine crackers

1. Arrange lettuce slices on plates.
2. Top with salmon, onion rings, and lemon wedge.
3. Cut the cream cheese slices into triangles and add to the plate.
4. Sprinkle capers on top and serve with bread or crackers.

A favorite at Rudy's restaurants for eighteen years!

Honey Vinaigrette Salad Dressing
Makes 3 cups

1-1/2 cups blended salad oil
3/4 cup malted vinegar
3 tablespoons minced garlic
1/4 cup honey
1-1/2 teaspoons Dijon mustard
1 teaspoon dried dill weed
1 teaspoon dried oregano
1 teaspoon dried marjoram

1. Blend all ingredients with a wire whisk until thoroughly combined.
2. Serve at room temperature over a bed of chilled mixed greens

This is a very simple, yet elegant, dish. Since it takes many pounds of beef bones and many hours of reduction, you probably don't have a supply of demi-glace at home. If you must, you may substitute Knorr demi-glace mix, and additional beef stock to make up 2 cups.

Veal Calvados
Serves 4

4 veal cutlets
Salt
Flour
6 tablespoons
  clarified butter
2 cups demi-glace
2 cooking apples,
  peeled, cored, and sliced
4 large mushrooms, sliced
1/2 cup Calvados

1. Pound veal cutlets with a meat-tenderizing mallet until thin.
2. Sprinkle with salt and then dredge in flour.
3. Add butter to a large saute pan and cook veal on high heat for several minutes, flipping to cook on both sides. Drain all butter from the pan.
4. Add demiglace, cover, and cook approximately 2 minutes.
5. Uncover and add apple slices, mushrooms, and Calvados. Cook for an additional 3 or 4 minutes, until sauce is reduced by about half.
6. Place cutlets in the middle of individual plates with the apple slices and mushrooms on one side and Glazed Leeks and Rhubarb on the other (recipe follows). Pour remaining sauce on top of veal.
7. Serve while hot.

*Tired of the same old vegetables? This recipe will wake up your
taste buds and make you wish you'd tried this years ago!*

Glazed Leeks and Rhubarb
Serves 4

2 medium leeks
2 stalks rhubarb
3 tablespoons butter
1/2 cup brown sugar
1/4 cup malt vinegar

1. Trim unhealthy greens from leeks. Slice leeks lengthwise and wash well to remove all grit. Wash rhubarb.
2. Cut leeks and rhubarb into 1-inch chunks.
3. Saute leeks in melted butter over low heat for about 15 minutes or until they begin to soften.
4. Add rhubarb, sugar, and vinegar. Cover and cook an additional 5 minutes. Uncover and cook another 5 minutes.
5. Serve while hot with entree.

This strudel will melt in your mouth! Folding the pastry over the apples requires a little dexterity, so borrow an extra pair of hands if you want a little insurance.

Rudy's Apple Strudel
Serves 4 to 6

5 medium apples, peeled,
  cored, and sliced
3/4 cup honey
3/4 cup brown sugar
1/4 teaspoon cinnamon
1/4 teaspoon nutmeg
1/4 teaspoon allspice
1/4 teaspoon vanilla extract
3/4 cup unseasoned bread crumbs
1 sheet puff pastry dough,
  properly thawed
1 egg
1 tablespoon water

1. Preheat oven to 350 degrees.
2. Combine apples, honey, brown sugar, cinnamon, nutmeg, allspice, vanilla and breadcrumbs in a large bowl. Stir well to combine.
3. Roll out puff pastry on floured surface until approximately 10" x 15".
4. Place apple mixture along the long edge of the puff pastry. Fold pastry over apple mixture two times. Seal ends with a fork.
5. Combine egg and water to form an egg wash. Brush the egg wash over the strudel. Prick holes into the top of the strudel every 4 or 5 inches to allow steam to escape.
6. Bake for approximately 35 to 40 minutes until apples are tender and pastry is golden brown.
7. Serve while still warm.

FLOOD TIDE RESTAURANT

Perched atop a hill overlooking the water, the Flood Tide Restaurant has been delighting patrons with its international and American cuisine for 30 years. This elegant establishment offers a complete dining experience—from the splendid view to the tableside preparation of dishes like their famous Caesar Salad and Bananas Foster. The Sunday brunch at Flood Tide has also gained a bit of a reputation over the years for its sumptuous buffet.

Executive Chef, Robert Tripp, a graduate of the Culinary Institute of America, who has had the honor of cooking for President Reagan, has shared with us some of these culinary treats.

Flood Tide Restaurant
at The Inn at Mystic
Routes 1 and 27
Mystic, CT 06355

Telephone: 203-536-8140

Credit Cards Accepted: American Express,
Carte Blanche, Diners Club, Discover, MasterCard, Visa

Flood Tide Restaurant Menu

Lobster Madeira Crepes
Caesar Salad
Grilled Salmon with Galliano Buerre Blanc
Grilled Herbed Summer Squash
Bananas Foster

Wine with Appetizer: California Semillon
Wine with Entree: California Chardonnay

What a heavenly way to start off a meal!

Lobster Madeira Crepes
Serves 6

2 tablespoons butter
8 mushrooms, thinly-sliced
1 tablespoon fresh shallots,
   finely chopped
1 tablespoon fresh parsley,
   finely chopped
3 ounces Madeira wine
12 ounces heavy cream
12 ounces fresh lobster meat,
   cooked and picked
6 crepes (recipe follows)
Fresh dillweed sprigs

1. Melt butter and saute mushrooms for 3 minutes at medium-high heat to brown slightly.
2. Add shallots and parsley and continue to saute for 30 seconds.
3. Add wine and scrape pan to incorporate browned bits. Allow liquid to reduce until most of liquid is gone.
4. Add heavy cream and continue to reduce until the liquid coats the back of a spoon slightly. Add lobster meat just to heat through.
5. Divide the filling among the 6 crepes and roll up, reserving a little sauce for the top of each. Garnish with sprigs of fresh dill.
6. Serve immediately.

Explaining how to make crepes takes far more energy than actually making them. The first one or two may indicate that you need to adjust the thickness of the batter or the amount of heat under the pan. Don't worry if they don't look perfect because they will be rolled up and topped with sauce. Enjoy leftover crepes with fruit compote or maple syrup at breakfast!

Crepes
Makes 10 crepes

2 extra-large eggs
1 to 1-1/4 cups milk
1 pinch salt
1 cup flour
4 to 5 tablespoons
    butter, melted

1. Beat eggs in a small bowl until smooth with a wire whisk.
2. Add 1 cup milk and salt and then mix in flour until batter is smooth. Add 2 tablespoons melted butter while stirring.
3. If time permits, cover the bowl with plastic wrap and let sit at room temperature for 2 to 3 hours (or in refrigerator for up to 12 hours).
4. When you are ready to cook the crepes, add up to 1/4 cup milk if mixture is thicker than heavy cream.
5. Heat an omelet pan at medium-high heat and use about 1/2 teaspoon melted butter per crepe. Pour approximately 1/4 cup of batter into pan, rotating the pan to spread evenly.
6. Cook for about 15 to 20 seconds on the first side and flip over. Cook for approximately 15 seconds on the other side. Remove from pan and repeat process. Crepes should be relatively pale and supple to facilitate rolling.
7. Crepes may be made ahead and stored tightly-wrapped in the refrigerator. Rewarm before using in recipes, taking care not to dry them out.

There is nothing quite like a Caesar salad prepared at your table!

Caesar Salad
Serves 6

30 to 40 grinds of freshly-ground
　black pepper
1 tablespoon ground anchovy
5 to 6 large garlic cloves
1/2 lemon
3 egg yolks
6 ounces olive oil
1 large head romaine lettuce,
　cut in 1 inch strips.
1 cup croutons
1/4 cup grated Parmesan cheese

1. Combine black pepper and anchovy in wooden salad bowl.
2. Using a garlic press, squeeze the juice from the garlic cloves into the above mixture.
3. Squeeze in enough lemon juice to moisten the above mixture and stir with a dinner fork.
4. Add raw egg yolks and blend with the fork to incorporate all ingredients well.
5. Add oil while feverishly whipping with the fork to create a mayonnaise-like consistency.
6. Add lettuce and toss with the dressing.
7. Sprinkle with croutons and Parmesan cheese and serve.

Broiled or grilled fish is one of the fastest and easiest dishes to prepare.
The Galliano Buerre Blanc turns this basic dish into a masterpiece.

Grilled Salmon with Galliano Buerre Blanc
Serves 6

2 tablespoons orange zest
1 tablespoon fresh parsley,
   chopped
1 tablespoon fresh shallots,
   choppped
1 tablespoon butter
Juice from 2 oranges
2 ounces Galliano liquor
3 ounces heavy cream
7 tablespoons butter
6 8-ounce pieces of salmon fillet

1. Preheat broiler.
2. Saute orange zest, parsley, and shallots in 1 tablespoon butter.
3. Add orange juice and Galliano and reduce liquid by half.
4. Add cream and reduce liquid by half again. Remove from heat and stir in 7 tablespoons butter. Keep Galliano Butter warm until time to serve.
5. Broil the salmon until flesh flakes easily (3 to 10 minutes depending on thickness).
6. Top with sauce and serve immediately.

If you are entertaining someone who doesn't usually like vegetables,
try this recipe. Everything done on a grill tastes great!

Grilled Herbed Summer Squash
Serves 6

3/4 cup olive oil
1/2 teaspoon dried oregano
1/2 teaspoon dried thyme
1/2 teaspoon dried basil
1 clove garlic, minced
3 medium summer squash,
   washed and cut diagonally

1. Gently heat olive oil, oregano, thyme, basil, and garlic over medium-low heat until warmed through, about 5 minutes.
2. Cool 3 hours at room temperature.
3. Dip squash in the oil and place on preheated grill. You may want to use a grilling "basket" to facilitate basting and flipping and to prevent squash from falling into the coals.
4. Baste frequently while grilling for approximately 2 minutes on each side, until slightly tender.
5. Serve hot with entree.

In New Orleans "voodoo dust" is sprinkled into the flames of this classic dessert. It is said to be dust scraped from the brick grave of Marie Laveau, the infamous Voodoo Queen. In reality, "voodoo dust" is just a pinch of cinnamon that sparks in the flames, but it makes a great story when you are entertaining. (Keep your cinnamon in a jeweler's ring box for special effect.) Note: When you're ready to flame this dessert, ignite a small amount of liquor in a long-handled ladle and then light the rest of the dish with the ladle. You then greatly reduce the risk of burning your hand.

Bananas Foster
Serves 6

6 tablespoons butter
7 rounded tablespoons
  light brown sugar
Juice from 1 orange
2 ounces creme de banana
2 tablespoons walnuts,
  chopped
4 bananas, sliced 1/4 inch thick,
  diagonally
2 ounces Captain Morgan spiced rum
6 large scoops vanilla ice cream

1. Combine butter and brown sugar in a skillet over medium heat and carmelize.
2. Add orange juice and creme de banana and flame, aggitating pan slightly.
3. Add walnuts, bananas, and rum and flame again, aggitating pan slightly.
4. Put ice cream into individual bowls and spoon equal amounts of banana mixture on top.
5. Serve while warm.

HARBORVIEW RESTAURANT

Over the past twenty years Harborview has earned a reputation for the finest French cuisine in the area. It is the ultimate romantic dining experience with candlelit tables in the stately dining room overlooking moon-washed Stonington Harbor. Exceptional service is de rigueur whether you are seated in the main dining room or the famous Harborview bar where lighter fare is served. The Sunday brunch is a magnificent buffet of French and Continental dishes that will keep you coming back for more.

Harborview Restaurant
60 Water Street
Stonington, CT 06378

203-535-2720

Credit Cards Accepted: American Express,
Diners Club, MasterCard, Visa

Harborview Restaurant
Menu

Wild Mushrooms in Filo with
Roasted Garlic Cream Sauce
Calalloo Crabmeat Soup
Sole en Papillotes
Chocolate Decadence

Wine with Appetizer: French St. Veran
Wine with Entree: Oregon Pinot Gris

An exotic appetizer of this magnitude is sure to impress, and besides that, it tastes great!

Wild Mushrooms in Filo with Roasted Garlic Cream Sauce
Serves 6

10 ounces fresh wild mushrooms
8 ounces fresh, white mushrooms
4 tablespoons butter
1 teaspoon fresh basil, finely diced
1 shallot, finely diced
Salt
Freshly-ground black pepper
4 tablespoons brandy
6 sheets filo dough, properly thawed
12 tablespoons butter, melted
Chives for garnish

1. Preheat oven to 350 degrees.
2. Wash, drain, and chop all mushrooms.
3. Melt 4 tablespoons butter in saucepan and saute mushroom mixture with basil and shallot. Cook until mushrooms are limp and shallot is translucent. Season to taste with salt and pepper. Add brandy and cook for several minutes to reduce liquid.
4. Place 1 filo sheet on table and brush with melted butter. Top with second filo sheet and lightly butter. Place third filo sheet and lightly butter.
5. On the long edge of 3 filo sheets, place 6 piles of the mushroom mixture. Cut between the piles and fold the dough over the mushrooms into triangles, as if folding a flag. Trim off any excess. Repeat process with remaining 3 sheets of filo.

6. Lightly butter the top of the triangles and place on lightly greased baking sheet. Bake for approximately 10 minutes, until golden brown.
7. Spread a little Roasted Garlic Cream Sauce on a plate and top with 2 filo triangles on each.
8. Garnish with chives and serve immediately.

You'll be tempted to lick your plate clean with this sauce, but please try to conform to acceptable social standards.

Roasted Garlic Cream Sauce

2 cloves garlic, unpeeled
2 cups heavy cream
1/4 cup beef consomme
1/2 bay leaf
Salt
Freshly ground black pepper

1. Preheat oven to 350 degrees.
2. Roast garlic in oven approximately 20 minutes, until golden brown inside. Peel garlic cloves when cool enough to handle.
3. Combine all ingredients in a heavy saucepan. Bring to almost a boil. Lower heat and reduce to approximately 1-1/4 cups of sauce, approximately 20 to 30 minutes, being careful not to boil over. Remove bay leaf.
4. Puree sauce and pass through fine cheesecloth. Season to taste with salt and pepper.
5. Keep warm until ready to serve.

The cream, crabmeat, and coconut milk form a tasty alliteration punctuated by the bright green spinach-- sure to make your best-sellers list.

Calalloo Crabmeat Soup
Serves 8

1/2 onion, finely diced
4 tablespoons olive oil
2 cloves garlic, minced
1 bay leaf
2 quarts heavy cream
1 10-ounce can chicken consomme
1 13-ounce can coconut milk
1 cup coarsely chopped spinach,
   stems removed
8 ounces crabmeat
Salt
White pepper to taste

1. Saute onion in olive oil over medium heat until translucent. Add garlic and saute for a minute longer. Add bay leaf.
2. Stir in heavy cream, chicken consomme, and coconut milk to combine. Reduce over medium-high heat until it is the consistency of a cream soup (20-60 minutes depending on the level of heat under the pot), stirring frequently and taking care not to let soup boil over. Reduce heat.
3. In a separate pan, drop spinach into boiling water and drain immediately. Add spinach to the soup and then the crabmeat, just to heat through. Season to taste with salt and white pepper.
4. Serve while hot.

These parchment bundles hold a complete meal in themselves. You can accomplish the same taste using aluminum foil, but the fun is in the drama of peeling open the beautifully browned parchment.

Sole en Papillotes
Serves 6

12-18 small red potatoes, torn
   (peeled around the middle to form 6 or 7 sides)
8 ounces whipped butter
2 shallots, minced, poached, and drained
1 teaspoon chervil
1 teaspoon parsley, chopped
1 teaspoon green peppercorns
Salt and pepper to taste
6 pieces of parchment approximately 16" x 16"
18 pieces of sole (about 2-1/4 pounds)
12 ounces Brie, cut into 18 thin slices
3 carrots, peeled and julienned
1 or 2 small yellow squash, julienned
1 or 2 small zucchini, julienned

1. Preheat oven to 350 degrees.
2. Boil the potatoes for about 10 minutes until able to be pierced with a toothpick, but not cooked so well that they are starting to fall apart. Drain and set aside.
3. Combine whipped butter, shallots, chervil, parsley, peppercorns, salt and pepper. (This can be made ahead and refrigerated.)
4. Fold parchment in half and draw 6 half-heart shapes as big as the parchment pieces. Cut out the "hearts".
5. Fold the pieces of sole over the slices of Brie, with the skin side in.

6. Arrange 3 pieces of sole in the center of one side of each heart. Place two or three potatoes around the sole. Divide the julienned vegetables among the 6 hearts. Top each serving with whipped herbed butter. Fold the top half of the parchment over.

7. Starting at the top of the heart, narrowly fold the parchment sides over twice and crimp together all the way to the point of the heart. Place on cookie sheets and bake about 20 minutes until the fish and vegetables are cooked through. (You **cannot** open the bundles to peek and reseal them.)

8. Serve one browned parchment bundle on each plate while hot.

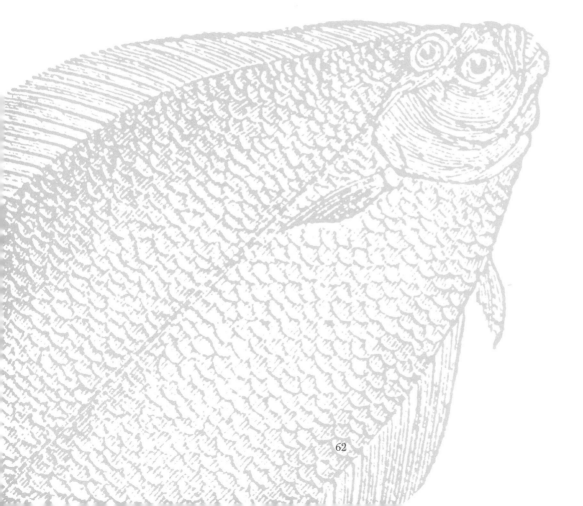

There are times when you have to cut loose and forget about fat and cholesterol. Life is too short not to enjoy life's little pleasures—in moderation, of course. This dessert is reserved for Chocoholics only.

Chocolate Decadence
Serves 8 or more

Cake:
12 ounces bittersweet chocolate, melted
12 ounces unsalted butter, softened
6 eggs
1-1/2 cups plus 2 tablespoons sugar
6 tablespoons cornstarch, sifted

1. Preheat oven to 350 degrees. Lightly grease two 9" x 13" x 2" pans. Cut parchment paper to fit and place on pans.
2. Place melted chocolate in a mixer with a paddle. Slowly add butter and then beat on high speed until light and fluffy.
3. In another bowl cream the eggs and sugar together until light and fluffy.
4. Add chocolate mixture to sugar mixture at slow speed. Add cornstarch just to incorporate.
5. Spread batter evenly on two pans.
6. Bake for approximately 20 minutes. Cake will rise during baking. A light crust is desired, though cake should still be moist inside. Cake will fall when removed from oven. Cool and remove parchment.

Butter Cream:

6 egg yolks
1/2 cup sugar
1/4 cup water
10 ounces bittersweet chocolate,
  melted
1 pound unsalted butter
Approximately 4 ounces
  semi-sweet chocolate

1. Cream yolks until light and fluffy.
2. While eggs are being beaten mix sugar and water together in a small sauce pan. Bring to a boil and continue boiling for 3 minutes. Let cool slightly.
3. When egg yolks are ready add sugar mixture in a slow steady stream while the mixer is on slow speed. Mix until eggs are cool. Add chocolate and then add butter slowly. Mix on high speed until light and fluffy.
4. In a double boiler slowly melt semi-sweet chocolate and set aside.

To assemble:

1. Cut the cakes into halves, lengthwise, making 4 long, narrow pieces of cake.
2. Place a thin layer of butter cream on the top of 1 layer of cake.
3. Continue alternating cake and butter cream layers. Fill in any holes with remaining butter cream.
4. Refrigerate cake until set. Trim to even sides if necessary. Cover top with a thin layer of melted chocolate.
5. Let set and then slice into serving portions. Makes 1 cake approximately 13" long and 4-1/2" wide.

J. P. Daniels

Located just outside Mystic, J. P. Daniels offers its renowned cuisine and service in the relaxed country setting of an historic, post and beam barn. Known as "where locals choose to dine", this is a completely non-smoking establishment. A recently-instituted new menu emphasizing lighter cuisine offers an extensive selection of delicious entrees, appetizers, and desserts. The owners also welcome "grazing", which is defined as "the fine art of dining on selected appetizers, pasta, and a choice salad". Another option here is the sumptuous Sunday Brunch buffet. No matter which approach you prefer, you'll enjoy this thoughtful restaurant with complete children's menu and very competitive pricing. Recapture this dining experience at home using the following recipes.

J. P. Daniels
Route 184
Gold Star Highway
Old Mystic, CT 06372

Telephone: 203-572-9564

Credit Cards Accepted: American Express, MasterCard, Visa

J. P. Daniels
Menu

Baked Escargot with Parsley Butter
Sherried Mushroom Soup
Strawberry Marguerita Sorbet
Broiled Scallops a la J. P. Daniels
Vanilla Souffles with Fresh Fruit and Armagnac Sauce

Wine with Appetizer: French Pouilly Fuisse
Wine with Entree: French Sancerre

This is a very exotic dish, of course. If you don't have the escargot shells needed, substitute large pasta shells cooked al dente and then you can eat the whole thing!

Baked Escargot with Parsley Butter
Serves 6

24 burgundy snails, canned
   and shells to bake them in
2 tablespoons unsalted butter
1-1/2 tablespoons chopped shallots
1-1/2 cups dry white wine
Salt
Freshly-ground black pepper
5 slices white bread

1. Drain the snails well.
2. Melt butter in a sauce pan and add the shallots. Saute until tender.
3. Add wine. Season to taste with salt and pepper. Add snails and simmer approximately 20 to 25 minutes to tenderize. Remove from heat.
4. Remove the crusts from the bread and process in a food processer until bread is reduced to small crumbs.
5. Preheat oven to 400 degrees.
6. Place snails in shells and pack with the parsley butter (recipe follows). Sprinkle the bread crumbs on top.
7. Bake for 8 to 10 minutes or until escargot are heated through.
8. Serve immediately.

Hazelnut powder can be produced by processing hazelnuts in a food processor until flour-like in consistency. If you have butter leftover, it is also delicious used with mushrooms, potatoes, etc.

Parsley Butter

1-2/3 cups unsalted butter
1 bunch parsley, chopped
1-1/2 tablespoons minced garlic
2-1/2 tablespoons minced shallots
1/2 cup hazelnut powder
1 tablespoon salt
Freshly-ground pepper

1. Place butter in a mixer and beat until creamy and smooth.
2. Add the parsley, garlic, shallots, hazelnut powder , salt, and pepper. Mix thoroughly.

The sherry contributes a delicate flavor to this soup.
This is not a thick, heavy soup, so you will have room for the rest of your meal.

Sherried Mushroom Soup
Serves 6 to 8

3 tablespoons butter
1/2 cup carrots, finely diced
1/2 cup celery, finely diced
3/4 cup onions, diced
20 ounces fresh mushrooms, sliced
3 tablespoons flour
1 quart chicken stock
1-1/2 teaspoons dried thyme
1 bay leaf
1/2 teaspoon dried rosemary
1/2 cup cream sherry
2 cups half and half

1. Melt butter in a large soup pot over medium heat and add carrots and celery. Saute about 10 minutes and then add onions. Saute 5 minutes more. Vegetables should be just tender at this point.
2. Add mushrooms, mixing well and cook, covered, for about 10 minutes until tender.
3. Stir in flour and cook 3 minutes. Stir in chicken stock and add thyme, bay leaf, and rosemary. Bring to a boil.
4. Add sherry and half and half. Cook until heated through and serve with a dollop of creme fraiche. (To make, beat 1/2 cup whipping cream with 3 tablespoons sour cream for 30 seconds at low speed and let stand, covered, at room temperature for several hours or overnight until thickened, stirring once or twice. Refrigerate until ready to use; will last one week.)

A delicious way to cleanse your palate between courses, it may also be used as a dessert. See the mail order sources section if you can't find an ice cream maker locally. I recommend the type that uses no electricity, salt, or ice. It's a great way to use up overripe fruit, juices, etc.

Strawberry Marguerita Sorbet
Serves 8 or more

1 cup granulated sugar
2 cups hot water
32 ounces of frozen strawberries, thawed
6 to 8 tablespoons fresh lime juice
6 tablespoons tequila
1/4 cup triple sec
Approximately 6 cups sliced fresh fruits
such as papaya, mango, pineapple, or kiwi
1 bunch fresh mint sprigs

1. In a saucepan dissolve sugar in hot water over medium heat. Let cool.
2. In a blender puree berries. Mix in 6 tablespoons lime juice.
3. Add the sugar syrup into the berry mixture, blend, and add more lime juice to taste, if necessary.
4. Refrigerate until well chilled.
5. Process in an ice cream maker, thoroughly incorporating tequila and triple sec near the end of the processing.
6. Freeze in covered container for several hours to mellow flavors.
7. Allow to soften slightly in refrigerator before serving.
8. To serve, place scoops of sorbet in center of plates and surround with fresh fruit.
9. Garnish with mint sprigs and serve immediately.

Sometimes the simple dishes are the best. This is ready to serve in next to no time.

Scallops a la J. P. Daniels
Serves 4

2 pounds sea scallops
2 tablespoons butter, melted
2 tablespoons lemon juice
Salt and freshly-ground black pepper
1 cup seasoned breadcrumbs
1 teaspoon Dijon mustard
3 slices of bacon, chopped and cooked

1. Combine scallops, butter, lemon juice, and salt and pepper to taste in an ovenproof pan.
2. Broil 3 to 5 minutes until scallops are just done and transfer scallops and liquid to an oven-proof serving dish.
3. Combine bread crumbs, mustard, and bacon in a separate bowl.
4. Sprinkle over scallops and broil again just for a few seconds to brown the topping.
5. Serve while hot with your favorite starch and vegetable.

If you're looking for an unusual dessert, this is it. Vanilla sugar is sugar and vanilla beans that have been stored together in a jar in a cool place for a week or more. Note: Use care when removing souffle cups from the hot water.

Vanilla Souffles with Fresh Fruit and Armagnac Sauce
Serves 6

3 tablespoons butter, softened
1/2 cup superfine sugar
2 tablespoons flour
6 tablespoons cold milk
1/2 cup vanilla sugar
5 egg yolks, room temperature
1 tablespoon vanilla
4 egg whites, room temperature

1. Preheat oven to 350 degrees. and brush inside 6 souffle cups with 1 tablespoon softened butter. Coat with a layer of sugar and chill.
2. Melt 2 tablespoons butter in a non-aluminum saucepan. Whisk in the flour and cook over low heat for about 1 minute. Remove from heat.
3. Add cold milk and return to heat. Boil for 2 to 3 minutes, whisking constantly.
4. Pour milk mixture into large bowl and mix in the remaining superfine sugar and the vanilla sugar.
5. Separate the eggs and store the egg whites and the bowl in which they will be beaten in the refrigerator until ready to use.
6. In a separate bowl whisk the egg yolks until thick and lemony. Add a small amount of the milk mixture to the yolks to warm them up. Then slowly add all the yolk mixture to the milk mixture Stir in the vanilla.
7. In a separate bowl beat the egg whites until stiff peaks are formed. Gently fold the egg whites into the egg yolk mixture, being careful not to deflate them.

8. Divide mixture into 6 souffle cups. Place cups in a baking pan, adding water so that it comes half way up the sides of the souffle cups.
9. Bake for 20 minutes or until cake tester comes out clean.
10. Run a knife around edges and unmold onto dessert plates covered in the fresh fruit and armagnac sauce (recipe follows). Serve immediately as souffles tend to deflate the longer they sit around.

This tangy sauce may be made in advance and stored in the refrigerator. Rewarm before serving. Try to save it for the souffles, or ice cream, or pound cake, or . . .etc.

Fresh Fruit and Armagnac Sauce

6 fresh apricots
2 large peaches
1-1/2 cups fresh strawberries, sliced
2 cups fresh raspberries
1 cup superfine sugar
Juice of 2 lemons
6 tablespoons Armagnac (a cognac)

1. Drop apricots and peaches into boiling water for about 20 seconds, just to loosen skins. Peel apricots and peaches and cube.
2. In a large skillet place the apricots, peaches, strawberries, raspberries, sugar, and lemon juice. Cook for about 10 minutes over medium-high heat until slightly thickened; remove from heat, and let cool.
3. Stir in Armagnac and serve with vanilla souffles.

THE MOORING

The Mooring in the Mystic Hilton is one of Mystic's finest restaurants, having won praise from local and regional food critics. Executive Chef, Paul Zenga and his staff take great pride in the cuisine which you'll find to be creative and flavorful without being intimidating. Menus change with the season to take advantage of the freshest ingredients available, and it is always exciting to see what imaginative dishes will be offered next. Because of the wide variety of selections, you may have trouble deciding! Since The Mooring is open for breakfast, lunch, or dinner, you will have ample opportunity to sample fine dishes all day long! It's easy to find, located opposite Mystic Aquarium.

The Mooring
at the Mystic Hilton
Coogan Boulevard
Mystic, CT 06355

Telephone: 203-572-0731

Credit Cards Accepted: American Express,
Diners Club, Discover, MasterCard, Visa

The Mooring
Menu

Duck Strudel with Plum Mint Sauce
Black Bean Soup
Tournedos of Beef Dijonnaise with Wild Mushrooms
Frozen Grand Marnier Souffle

Wine with Appetizer: French Beaujolais-Village
Wine with Entree: Napa Valley Cabernet Sauvignon

Don't be afraid to try strudels! Frozen filo dough is easy to use; just keep it covered with plastic wrap or a damp dishtowel to prevent it from drying out. This is a wonderful way to start a special meal. It's also delicious with boneless pork if duck isn't readily available.

Duck Strudel with Plum Mint Sauce
Serves 4

2 4-ounce duck breasts
1 tablespoon sesame oil
1 small red onion, julienned
1/2 white onion, julienned
1/2 teaspoon garlic, chopped
1/2 teaspoon shallot, chopped
1 large carrot, julienned
2 scallions (green part only),
   cut on angle
1 tablespoon sesame seeds
1 tablespoon light soy sauce
1 tablespoon white wine
1/2 teaspoon cornstarch
Black pepper to taste
8 sheets filo dough, properly thawed
4 tablespoons butter, melted

1. Preheat oven to 425 degrees.
2. Roast duck breast, fat side up for 15 minutes or until rare to medium rare. Allow to cool, remove fat, and slice a quarter inch thick. Lay slices flat and cut into quarter inch matchsticks, julienne style. Reduce oven temperature to 350 degrees.
3. Over medium-high heat, heat sesame oil in a saute pan. Do not let this smoke. Add onions and saute for approximately 3 minutes. Add garlic,

shallots, and carrots. Cook until carrots are tender, but firm. Add scallions, sesame seeds, soy sauce, and duck. Cook for 2 minutes.

4. Mix wine and cornstarch in a bowl and add to duck mixture. Season to taste with black pepper. Let mixture cool until lukewarm.
5. Place one sheet of filo on a cutting board. Brush with melted butter and place another sheet on top.
6. Divide the duck mixture into 4 equal parts. Place one part in an elongated mound in the center of the filo. Slowly roll the filo and duck stuffing up in jelly-roll style. Fold under 1-1/2 inches of dough at each end. Brush with butter and place on a baking sheet. Repeat process to form 4 strudels.
7. Bake for 5 to 7 minutes at 350 degrees or until golden brown.
8. Place strudels on cutting board with a spatula and cut each strudel diagonally into 3 pieces.
9. Drizzle some plum mint sauce (recipe follows) on four small plates, arrange strudel on each plate, and drizzle tops with more sauce. Serve warm.

An exotic appetizer like duck strudel demands an imaginative sauce such as this.

Plum Mint Sauce

5 ripe plums of any variety, peeled and pitted
4 sprigs of mint
1/4 cup white wine
2 tablespoons Knorr powdered demi-glace
1 cup cranberry juice
1/2 cup brown sugar

1. Puree the plums in a food processor. Add the mint and continue to process.
2. Put the puree in a saucepan and bring it to a light simmer with white wine.
3. Add the demi-glace powder, cranberry juice, and brown sugar.
4. Simmer over medium heat to reduce liquid until sauce is slightly thickened.

*You'll find this to be an especially flavorful, hearty
soup reminiscent of chili, and so easy to make!*

Black Bean Soup
Serves 6

1 medium red onion, diced
1 tablespoon minced garlic
1 large tomato, chopped (about 3/4 cup)
1 ounce bacon fat
1/2 teaspoon black pepper
1 teaspoon cumin
3/4 teaspoon chili powder
1/2 teaspoon curry powder
2 quarts of chicken stock
1-1/4 cups dried black beans, rinsed

1. Saute onion, garlic, and tomato in bacon fat in soup pot.
2. Add pepper, cumin, chili powder, curry powder, chicken stock, and beans.
3. Simmer until beans are tender, approximately 2 hours or so, stirring occasionally.
4. Serve hot.

This entree is not for the faint-hearted. This rich, robust fare
is perfectly complemented by a full-bodied cabernet. Enjoy!

Tournedos of Beef Dijonnaise with Wild Mushrooms
Serves 4

1 cup brandy
1-1/2 teaspoons minced shallot
1-1/2 teaspoons minced garlic
2 tablespoons Knorr demi-glace powder
2 cups water
1 tablespoon Dijon mustard
1 cup heavy cream
2 tablespoons butter
Salt and freshly-ground pepper
8 ounces morels or shitake mushrooms
8 4-ounce beef tenderloin steaks
(Butcher will cut for you)

1. In a medium-sized saucepan reduce brandy, 1 teaspoon shallots, and 1 teaspoon garlic down to near dryness.
2. In a bowl combine demi-glace powder and water and then add to pan with brandy. Bring to a boil.
3. Reduce to a simmer and add mustard and cream. Return to boil.
4. Remove from heat and whip in 1 tablespoon butter. Season with salt and pepper. Keep warm until ready to serve.
5. In another pan saute remaining shallots and garlic in remaining butter. Add mushrooms and gently saute approximately 3 or 4 minutes until cooked through. Season with salt and pepper. Set aside.
6. Grill or pan-fry tenderloins with salt and pepper until cooked to your level of preference.
7. Spoon sauce on warm plates and top with two tenderloins and then mushrooms. Serve with your favorite vegetable and starch.

Just smile and say "thank you" when complimented on this dessert.
There is no need to confess how easy it was to make.

Frozen Grand Marnier Souffle
Serves 4

2 egg yolks
3 tablespoons sugar
1 tablespoon water
2 tablespoons Grand Marnier
3/4 cup plus 1 tablespoon
  heavy cream
Cocoa powder
Whipped cream for garnish
4 strawberries, cut to fan open

1. Whip egg yolks in medium bowl for 3 minutes.
2. In a sauce pan, heat sugar and water to a boil and continue to boil for 2 minutes, stirring constantly. This step is critical. You want to boil sugar just long enough to form a syrup. Boiling too long will cause the sugar to solidify.
3. Immediately fold sugar mixture into egg yolks and add Grand Marnier.
4. In a chilled bowl, whip heavy cream until underwhipped (peaks not formed yet).
5. Fold egg yolk mixture into whipped cream.
6. Pour into individual dessert glasses and freeze for 4 hours.
7. When serving, take out of freezer, dust with cocoa powder and garnish with whipped cream and strawberry "fans".

ONE SOUTH CAFE

Nestled by the town soccer fields and the railroad viaduct, just outside Stonington Borough, One South Cafe has a charming Victorian atmosphere which perfectly complements its distinctive fare. For ten years One South has held to the philosophy of offering the customer more options while utilizing only the finest and freshest ingredients. As a result, you can get anything from a great burger to a gourmet entree and everything is very reasonably priced. This restaurant is slightly off the beaten path, but well worth the effort to find it.

Owner Tricia Shipman has shared with us this selection of traditional recipes to recreate the flavors typical of the Portuguese fishing fleet home-ported in this enchanting village.

One South Cafe
201 North Main Street
Stonington, CT 06378

Telephone: 203-535-0418

Credit Cards Accepted: American Express, MasterCard, Visa

One South Cafe
Menu

Grilled Mussels
Portuguese Sausage and Vegetable Soup
Caldeirada
Classic Flan

Wine with Appetizer: French Muscadet
Wine with Entree: French Pommard

The Portuguese have always been closely linked to the sea. No matter which side of the Atlantic they sail, mussels are one of the fruits of their labor.

Grilled Mussels
Serves 6 to 8

5 pounds fresh mussels,
   scrubbed and de-bearded
2 teaspoons fresh minced garlic
1-1/2 tablespoon fresh parsley, chopped
3/4 pound butter, softened
3/4 teaspoon garlic powder
3/4 teaspoon white pepper
1-1/2 cups good-quality bread crumbs

1. Steam mussels until opened and remove top shells. Set aside.
2. Preheat broiler.
3. Incorporate garlic and half the parsley into softened butter.
4. In a separate bowl, mix garlic powder, pepper, and remaining parsley into the breadcrumbs.
5. Spread herbed butter generously onto mussel halves, covering completely.
6. Press buttered surface of the mussels into the breadcrumb mixture.
7. Place mussels on an ovenproof platter and broil until golden brown, about 3 to 5 minutes.
8. Serve immediately with crusty French or Italian bread.

*Here is one variation of a very popular traditional soup
using linguica, a rather lean and spicy Portuguese sausage.*

Portuguese Sausage and Vegetable Soup
Serves 8

1/4 cup olive oil
2 large onions, diced
6 stalks celery, sliced
1 tablespoon garlic, minced
1 tablespoon dried oregano
1-1/2 quarts chicken stock
2 cups crushed tomatoes
3 or 4 carrots, peeled and sliced
4 large potatoes, peeled and cubed
1-1/2 pounds linguica, cooked and sliced
   (see mail order sources)
1 small head cabbage or kale, chopped
1 tablespoon fresh parsley
Freshly-ground black pepper, to taste

1. Heat oil in a large heavy pot. Add onions and saute over low heat until translucent.
2. Add celery and cook a few minutes more.
3. Add garlic and oregano, stirring until aromatic.
4. Add chicken stock, tomatoes, carrots, and bring to a boil.
5. Add potatoes, linguica, and cabbage or kale. Continue cooking until potatoes are tender. Thin with additional stock or water, if necessary.
6. Sprinkle with parsley, season with pepper, and serve hot.

The French have Bouillabaisse; the Portuguese have Caldeirada. This is a great, hearty seafood stew prepared all along the Portuguese coast. We're glad it found its way to our shores!

Caldeirada
Serves 8

4 leeks, sliced lengthwise, washed, and trimmed
1/4 cup olive oil
3 cloves fresh garlic, minced
3 tablespoons cilantro, chopped
1 teaspoon coriander seed, crushed
1 to 3 teaspoon(s) saffron, to taste
1 cup rich fish stock or clam juice
3 28-ounce cans whole plum tomatoes
1 cup dry white wine
1 bay leaf
1 teaspoon dried oregano
Freshly-ground black pepper, to taste
3 to 4 pounds of one or more of the following seafoods:
    firm white fish (monkfish, cod, etc.), shrimp, scallops,
    clams or mussels in shells, lobster
Fresh pasta, cooked al dente (optional)

1. Chop leeks into 1/2-inch pieces.
2. Heat oil in a large saucepan. Add leeks and saute gently until softened.
3. Add garlic, cilantro, coriander, and saffron. Continue to cook about 3 minutes.
4. Add fish stock, tomatoes, wine, bay leaf, and oregano. Simmer for about 30 minutes; add pepper and taste to adjust seasonings.
5. Add seafood and simmer until just cooked through.
6. Serve in individual soup bowls or ladle over your favorite pasta.

Next to fresh fruit, the Portuguese prefer egg-rich dishes like flan and rice pudding for dessert. Here is a recipe for the classic flan, though it may also be flavored with orange, coffee or chocolate. To flavor with orange, simmer the milk with the peel of 1 orange and a 2" piece of cinnamon stick for 2 to 3 minutes. Remove from heat and let stand for 30 minutes. Pour the milk through a strainer before using in the recipe.

Pudim Flan
Serves 8

1 cup granulated sugar
1/4 cup water
4 medium eggs
2 egg yolks
1/2 cup granulated sugar
1-1/2 teaspoons vanilla extract
4 cups whole milk
1 cup heavy cream

1. Put 1 cup of sugar in a heavy, wide, shallow saucepan. Cook over medium-low heat until melted, stirring frequently. When sugar is completely melted, remove from heat.
2. Slowly add water carefully, stirring constantly with a long-handled wooden spoon.
3. Put back on heat and simmer until the sugar is the color of maple syrup.
4. Slowly pour just enough sugar to cover the bottom of 8 pyrex custard cups, rotating to assure coverage.
5. Place cups in 9" x 13" x 2" baking dish and carefully pour enough water in the baking dish to come up the sides of the pyrex cups 1 inch.
6. In a blender or large bowl combine eggs, yolks, 1/2 cup sugar, vanilla, milk, and cream. Pour into pyrex cups to within 1/2 inch of the tops.
7. Bake at 350 degrees about 1 hour. Test for doneness by inserting the blade

of a butter knife into the center. When it comes out clean, the flan is done.

8. Remove the cups from the water bath as soon as possible, as the custard will continue to cook while in the warm water. Allow to cool completely at room temperature and then refrigerate.

9. When ready to serve, run a knife around the edge of the cups. Place a dessert plate over each cup and invert.

Randall's Ordinary

In colonial times, an ordinary was a tavern and social center. Today, in North Stonington, the original farmhouse that was home to John Randall over 300 years ago is still being used to create a dining experience that is anything but ordinary. All the dishes on the menu are prepared on the open hearth and served by those in period costume. One 7:00 p.m. seating gives you time to come early and stroll the 27 acres of grounds and sample pre-dinner snacks and colonial libations in the tap room while your dinner finishes cooking on the hearth.

While the menu changes every day, innkeeper Cindy Clark offers this typical autumn menu of traditional tastes that you can create in your own kitchen, no matter how modern.

Randall's Ordinary
41 Norwich-Westerly Road
(Route 2)
North Stonington, CT 06378

Telephone: 203-599-4540

Credit Cards Accepted: American Express, MasterCard, Visa

Randall's Ordinary
Menu

Pumpkin Soup
Chicken and Oyster Pie
Minted Carrots
Three Sisters Rice
Bird's Nest Pudding

Wine with Entree: Connecticut Chardonnay

You'll be surprised at how quick, easy, and delicious this soup is —
the perfect opener on a chilly, autumn evening.

Pumpkin Soup
Serves 6

1/2 cup onions, chopped
3 tablespoons butter
1-3/4 cups fresh pumpkin
   puree or a 15-ounce can
1 teaspoon salt
1/4 teaspoon sugar
1/4 teaspoon freshly-grated nutmeg
1/4 teaspoon pepper
2-2/3 cups chicken broth
1/2 cup light cream
Chopped chives

1. Gently saute onions in melted butter in a large pan over medium heat until translucent.
2. Add pumpkin, salt, sugar, nutmeg, and pepper.
3. Slowly stir in chicken broth to incorporate and add cream. Simmer until heated through.
4. Serve while hot garnished with chives.

*Originating in colonial times, this is an interesting
combination of subtle flavors, punctuated with lemon.*

Chicken and Oyster Pie
Serves 6 to 8

1 pound boneless chicken breast,
    poached until just done
1 8-ounce can oysters or 12 fresh oysters,
    steamed until just opened
6 tablespoons butter
1/2 cup chopped celery
3 tablespoons flour
3/4 cup chicken broth
3/4 cup oyster or clam broth
1/2 cup light cream
1/2 teaspoon freshly-ground nutmeg
Juice of half a lemon
1/2 teaspoon grated lemon rind
Piecrust pastry for top crust
1 egg, beaten

1. Preheat oven to 400 degrees.
2. Cut chicken into bite-size chunks.
3. Drain oysters and reserve liquid.
4. Melt butter in large pan and saute celery until slightly tender. Stir in flour and cook for an additional 3 minutes to form roux. Add chicken and oyster broths, stirring constantly. Add cream and stir until thickened.
5. Add nutmeg, lemon juice and rind.
6. Place chicken and oysters in deep-dish 10" pie pan or shallow casserole. Pour sauce over and cover with pie crust. Pierce for vent holes and brush with egg.
7. Bake for 40 minutes and serve with carrots and rice (recipes follow).

If all vegetables tasted this good, there would be no need for desserts!

Minted Carrots
Serves 8

1-1/2 pounds carrots,
  peeled and julienned
1/3 cup water
1/2 teaspoon salt
3-1/2 tablespoons butter
1 cup heavy cream
2 tablespoons sugar
Freshly-ground black pepper,
  to taste
2 tablespoons fresh spearmint
  or peppermint
(1 tablespoon of dried mint
  may be subsituted.)

1. Combine carrots, water, and salt in saucepan. Bring to a boil and then reduce heat, cover, and cook slowly until carrots are almost tender, approximately 20 minutes. Drain any excess water from pan and add 1-1/2 tablespoons butter.
2. Heat cream in a separate saucepan until it just starts to come to a boil and pour over carrots. Simmer carrots in cream over medium-low heat approximately 15 minutes, uncovered, until carrots are tender and cream has been almost absorbed, stirring frequently.
3. Add 2 tablespoons softened butter, sugar, and pepper, mixing thoroughly. Add mint and serve hot with entree.

This recipe is Randall's adaptation of a Native American recipe. Corn, beans, and squash were the most important crops in the farming cultures of the Americas, providing the basis of a nutritious diet. The Iroquois referred to these major crops as the "Three Sisters".

Three Sisters Rice
Serves 6

1/2 pound wild rice
1 quart water
1 small onion, chopped
1-1/2 stalks celery, chopped
2 tablespoons butter
3 cups chicken broth, heated
2 cups squash, peeled and diced
　(butternut, acorn, or pumpkin)
1 cup corn kernels
8 ounces canned lima or
　pinto beans, drained
Ground thyme or sage, to taste

1. Soak the wild rice in water overnight.
2. Saute onion and celery in melted butter in a large pan.
3. Drain the rice and add to onion mixture. Stir in the heated broth and bring to a boil. Reduce heat and simmer, covered, for 45 to 60 minutes.
4. Add the diced squash for the last 20 minutes and cook until tender. Stir in the corn and beans at the end to just heat thorough.
5. Season to taste with thyme or sage or herbs of your choice.
6. Serve hot with entree.

If you like baked apples and custard, you'll love this dessert. Use only tart apples,however, or you'll get an excess of apple juice diluting the custard.

Bird's Nest Pudding
Serves 6 to 8

6 to 8 small, tart apples, unpeeled
Approximately 1 cup golden raisins
1/2 cup sugar
1-1/2 teaspoons flour
1-1/2 cups milk
3 eggs
Chopped walnuts
Grated nutmeg
Fresh whipped cream

1. Preheat oven to 350 degrees.
2. Core apples and place them in a shallow baking dish. Fill the centers with raisins.
3. Mix together the sugar, flour, milk, and eggs, and pour the mixture into the baking dish, being sure to get some of the liquid into the center of the apples.
4. Sprinkle walnuts and nutmeg over the top.
5. Bake for 60 minutes. Test that the apples are done and the custard is set. Bake up to an additional 15 minutes if necessary.
6. Serve warm with fresh whipped cream.

S. & P. OYSTER COMPANY

    S. & P. Oyster Company's riverfront location provides the ultimate convenience for boaters who can dock and dine. Ample parking and its proximity to the downtown shopping area and Mystic Seaport make it a convenient spot for everyone. No matter how you arrive, you'll enjoy the reasonably-priced lobster dinners, its trademark oysters, and wide-ranging menu that specializes in fresh seafood. S. & P. is housed in a beautiful building affording a view of the ever-changing activity on the river and the historic Mystic drawbridge. A children's menu is available making it an ideal restaurant for the whole family. The staff has provided us with a trio of seafood recipes for you to enjoy at home.

S. & P. Oyster Company
1 Holmes Street
Mystic, CT 06355

Telephone: 203-536-2674

Credit Cards Accepted: American Express,
Diners Club, MasterCard, Visa

S & P Oyster Company
Menu

Oysters Our Way
Clam Chowder
Swordfish Mediterranean
Chocolate Mousse

Wine with Appetizer: Brut Champagne
Wine with Entree: Spanish White Rioja

Oysters are difficult critters to shuck, but once its done, you'll be glad you did. A little fresh spinach (washed, picked, and chopped) just under the Swiss cheese is a nice option.

Oysters Our Way
Serves 6

24 oysters
2 tablespoons minced garlic
2 sticks softened butter
2 tablespoons dried parsley
1/4 pound Swiss cheese
1/2 cup bread crumbs

1. Preheat oven to 400 degrees.
2. Wash and shuck oysters, and rinse out shell fragments. Leave oysters in half shell.
3. Mix garlic, butter, and parsley together and add 1 teaspoon to each oyster. Bake for 5 to 7 minutes.
4. Top oysters with swiss cheese and bake until butter and cheese are melted, approximately 2 to 3 minutes.
5. Melt the remaining garlic butter mixture and mix bread crumbs into it, stirring to incorporate. Top oysters with buttered bread crumbs and continue baking until just browned.
6. Serve while hot.

*Hale and hearty, this is a soup to renew your spirits at the
end of a hard day. So substantial, it could be a meal in itself.*

Clam Chowder
Serves 6 to 8

1/4 pound bacon, chopped
3 stalks of celery, chopped
2 small Spanish onions, chopped
2 tablespoons garlic, minced
1-1/2 teaspoons dried thyme
1 teaspoon ground white pepper
1 teaspoon ground black pepper
1-1/2 teaspoons dried dillweed
2 10-ounce cans baby clams
1 10-ounce can minced clams
1 quart clam juice
3 medium potatoes, diced
2 quarts half and half
1/4 cup butter
1/4 cup flour

1. Saute bacon, celery, onions, garlic, thyme, peppers, and dillweed until onions become semi-translucent.
2. Add clams, clam juice and potatoes. Cook 10 minutes or so until potatoes are done.
3. Add half and half, simmering until heated through.
4. In a small pan melt butter and stir in flour. Cook for several minutes to form a roux and add to chowder in stages, until it is only slightly thickened.
5. Serve while still hot.

The combination of textures and tastes form a complexity
that will compel you to make this dish over and over again.

Swordfish Mediterranean
Serves 4

2 tablespoons seedless raisins
4 pieces of swordfish, about 6 ounces each
Flour for dredging
4 tablespoons olive oil
Salt and freshly-ground pepper, to taste
1 onion, chopped
1 stalk of celery, chopped
2 cloves of garlic, peeled and crushed
2 cups crushed tomatoes, (without peels, if fresh)
1/4 cup pignoli (pine nuts)
1 tablespoon capers, drained
3/4 cup black olives, sliced
2 bay leaves
Water or tomato juice

1. Preheat oven to 350 degrees.
2. Soak the raisins in lukewarm water for 15 minutes and then drain.
3. Coat the fish with flour.
4. Heat the oil in an oven-proof pan or casserole on top of the stove. Add the fish and brown on both sides. Drain on a brown paper bag and sprinkle with salt and pepper.
5. Add the onion, celery, and garlic to the pan and saute gently for 5 minutes. Add the tomatoes, salt, and pepper to taste and simmer, uncovered for 15 minutes.

6. Stir in the raisins, pignoli, capers, and olives and cook for an additional 5 minutes.
7. Return the fish to the pan, adding bay leaves and up to a cup of tomato juice or water to cover fish. Cover and bake for 15 to 20 minutes until the fish is tender.
8. Remove the fish from the pan and put the pan back on a stove burner. Let liquid reduce slightly while cooking over a medium-high flame.
9. Serve with your favorite pasta and vegetable.

The blending of coffee and chocolate makes this classic dessert a long-standing favorite. You'll be amazed at how easy it is to make.

Chocolate Mousse
Serves 8

3 ounces Maillards sweet chocolate
2 tablespoons extra-strong cold coffee
1 teaspoon instant coffee
4 eggs, separated
1/2 cup sugar
Pinch of salt
1-1/2 cups heavy cream

1. Melt the chocolate in the top of a double boiler.
2. Blend the coffees well and add to chocolate, stirring well. Set aside to cool.
3. Beat the egg yolks in a bowl until thick and lemony. Add the sugar and salt, and beat again until incorporated.
4. Add the chocolate mixture to the egg yolk mixture, mixing thoroughly.
5. Beat the egg whites until stiff and gently fold into the chocolate mixture.
6. Whip the heavy cream until stiff and fold into the chocolate mixture.
7. Spoon into a 2-quart mold or individual serving glasses. Chill 2 to 3 hours before serving.

Seahorse Restaurant

      Where do locals go for the freshest seafood and the best value? Seahorse Restaurant is the answer. It has been in existence for over 40 years and operated by John Hughes for the last ten. It is the kind of casual restaurant that brings people back over and over again, all year long. For a bit of local color and a great meal, take a trip to Noank, as quaint a New England village as you'll ever see. You'll be glad you did.

      Recreate this Italian menu with friends for a memorable evening.

Seahorse Restaurant
66 Marsh Road
(off Groton Long Point Road)
Noank, CT 06340

Telephone: 203-536-1670

Credit Cards Accepted: Discover, MasterCard, Visa

Seahorse Restaurant
Menu

Grilled Tuscan Bread with Scarmoza
Roasted Onion and Cannelini Soup
Pasta with Seafood and Lobster Butter
Sparagia alla Romana
Strawberries Amaretto

Wine with Appetizer: Italian Albana di Romagna
Wine with Entree: Santa Barbara Chardonnay

Simple, yet sophisticated, have your guests assemble this
appetizer while you attend to the rest of the meal.

Grilled Tuscan Bread with Scarmoza
Serves 6

12 slices 1" thick of
  Scala bread (Italian)
4 tablespoons virgin olive oil
1/2 cup roasted red peppers, chopped
1/4 cup Calamata black olives,
  pitted and chopped
6 basil leaves
6 slices Scarmoza (smoked mozzarella)

1. Preheat oven to 400 degrees.
2. Drizzle slices of bread with approximately half of the olive oil. Grill bread on both sides just long enough to mark grill stripes on it either under a broiler or over a gas, charcoal, or wood-fired grill.
3. Place bread on sheet pan and distribute roasted peppers, olives and basil leaves on bread slices.
4. Top with cheese and bake for approximately 10 to 15 minutes, until cheese is melted.
5. Serve with remaining oil drizzled on top.

The beans in this onion soup are a new twist that makes it tasty and good for you too!

Roasted Onion and Cannellini Soup
Serves 6

1/2 cup olive oil
2 medium onions,
  peeled and sliced
1/2 tablespoon garlic,
  chopped
1/2 teaspoon black pepper
1/2 teaspoon salt
1 teaspoon dried basil
1/2 teaspoon dried oregano
1 teaspoon sugar
2 quarts chicken stock
1 19-ounce can cannellini beans
  (white kidney)

1. In a medium size soup pot heat oil and brown onions, garlic, pepper, salt, basil, oregano and sugar over medium-low heat until onions are light brown, not black.
2. Add chicken stock and reduce for up to an hour over medium heat. Level of liquid should drop an inch or so.
3. Puree beans in their own juice in a food processer and add to soup. Simmer for an additional 30 minutes.
4. Serve hot.

The beautiful pink sauce and fresh seafood over pasta is the
ultimate taste treat. This is definately a dish for special occasions.

Pasta with Seafood and Lobster Butter
Serves 6

2 tablespoons butter
1 ounce fresh leeks, cut lengthwise,
  washed, and chopped
1/2 pound sea scallops
1 pound white shrimp,
  peeled and deveined
3 medium vine-ripened tomatoes,
  quartered
1/2 pound lobster meat,
  cooked and picked
1/2 tablespoon lobster base
2 cups heavy cream
Juice from half a lemon
1 cup blended Parmesan and
  Romano cheeses
Salt and Pepper to taste
6 servings of your favorite pasta,
  cooked al dente

1. In a large saucepan melt butter and saute leeks until translucent.
2. Add scallops, shrimp, and tomatoes and saute for 5 minutes.
3. Add lobster meat and lobster base and stir until thoroughly combined.
4. Add cream and lemon juice and simmer for 2 minutes. Add grated cheeses,
   stirring to incorporate. Season to taste with salt and pepper.
5. Serve immediately over hot pasta.

Icing the asparagus after blanching helps maintain the bright
green color and al dente texture for a wonderfully-fresh dish.

Sparagia alla Romana
Serves 6

18 small asparagus spears, cleaned
1/2 teaspoon freshly-ground black pepper
1 tablespoon fresh parsley, chopped
1/4 cup olive oil
Juice from 1 lemon
1/2 cup Pecorino Romano cheese

1. Preheat oven to 400 degrees.
2. Bring 2 quarts of water to a quick boil. Add asparagus and cook for 2 minutes. Remove from boiling water and soak in ice water.
3. Line up asparagus on a sheet pan and sprinkle with black pepper, parsley, oil, lemon juice and cheese.
4. Bake for 10 to 15 minutes until cheese is nicely browned.
5. Serve warm with entree.

There is nothing comparable to fresh strawberries in early summer floating on
billowy clouds of whipped cream. Amaretto is a distinctive addition.

Strawberries Amaretto
Serves 6

1 quart fresh strawberries,
    cleaned and halved
1/2 cup Amaretto di Saronno
2 tablespoons granulated sugar
2 cups heavy cream
1 teaspoon vanilla extract

1. Combine strawberries, Amaretto, and sugar in a bowl. Mix and refrigerate
    for at least 30 minutes.
2. In a medium mixing bowl combined cream and vanilla. Whip until smooth,
    semi-thick consistency.
3. Serve by placing whipped cream in the bottom of a dessert plate and
    placing strawberries on top. Drizzle some of the juice over the dessert.
    Serve immediately.

SEAMEN'S INNE RESTAURANT

The Seamen's Inne we know today was fashioned after a whaling captain's home, incorporating antiques, whaling artifacts, and building materials from the early Mystic settlement and neighboring tobacco farms. (The original Seamen's Inne was built in 1713.) Overlooking the Mystic River and wharves of Mystic Seaport, you'll enjoy the casual Samuel Adams Pub with 8 draught lagers and ales as well as several elegant fireplaced dining rooms.

The fare ranges from the deliciously simple to the simply delicious. Seasonal menus stress seafood and grilled items in the summer and heartier fare in the cooler weather. You won't want to miss the beauty of the decor and the traditional early American selections during the Christmas season. Be prepared to loosen your belt if you partake of the Dixieland Sunday brunch buffet. It's scrumptuous.

Seamen's Inne
105 Greenmanville Avenue
at the North Entrance of Mystic Seaport
Mystic, CT 06355

Telephone: 203-536-9649

Credit Cards Accepted: American Express, MasterCard, Visa

Seamen's Inne
Menu

Gazpacho
Seamen's Inne House Dressing
Seafood Pot Pie
Peach Cobbler

Wine with Entree: French Macon-Village

*Cool, crunchy, and spicy — the perfect summer soup to
beat the heat with and keep you away from the stove!*

Gazpacho
Serves 8

3 whole cucumbers,
  peeled and seeded
2 green peppers
1 large onion
2 whole carrots
2 stalks of celery
2 large tomatoes, diced
1 tablespoon chopped garlic
2 to 3 teaspoons black pepper, to taste
Dash of salt
1 quart tomato or vegetable juice
2 tablespoons wine vinegar
Sour cream for garnish
Fresh parsley sprigs for garnish

1. Finely chop cucumbers, peppers, onions, carrots, and celery and put in large bowl.
2. Add tomatoes, garlic, pepper, salt, juice, and vinegar. Mix thoroughly.
3. Chill well until serving time.
4. Garnish with dollop of sour cream and a sprig of parsley at serving time.

Pepper, cheese, and garlic dominate this substantial salad dressing.

Seamen's Inne House Dressing
Makes 2 cups

1 egg
1 cup salad oil
2 tablespoons plus 2 teaspoons
   wine vinegar
1/4 cup garlic powder
1/2 teaspoon salt
2 to 3 teaspoons black pepper
1 tablespoon dried oregano
1 tablespoon sugar
1/3 cup grated Romano cheese
Water, as needed

1. Break egg into mixer bowl and beat vigorously.
2. Slowly add oil until it starts to thicken. When mixture is as thick as mayonnaise, add vinegar, garlic powder, salt, pepper, oregano, sugar and cheese. Mix until smooth. Adjust thickness by adding up to several tablespoons of water.
3. Keep chilled until serving time.
4. Serve over a bed of your favorite mixed garden greens.

"Show stopper" is the only way to describe this very special seafood dish.
The flavor is subtle — the compliments won't be.

Seafood Pot Pie
Serves 8

9 tablespoons butter
1/2 cup flour
1 pound firm white fish
1 pound scallops
1 pound shrimp, peeled and deveined
2 Knorr fish bouillon cubes
1 Spanish onion, finely diced
1/2 cup sherry
1/2 cup half and half
1 teaspoon paprika
1 pound cooked lobster meat,
   cut into bite-sized pieces
(Don't forget to remove
   cartilage from claw meat)
1 or 2 sheets of puff pastry,
   properly thawed
1 egg
1 tablespoon water

1. Preheat oven to 400 degrees.
2. Melt 8 tablespoons butter in saucepan and stir in flour. Cook 5 minutes over low heat and set aside.
3. In a separate pan poach or steam fish until it flakes and remove with a slotted spoon. Use the same water to poach or steam scallops and shrimp until just done, approximately 3 minutes. Remove scallops and shrimp with

slotted spoon. Cut shrimp into bite-sized pieces, if necessary. Dissolve fish bouillon cubes in liquid and add enough water to make 1 quart. Set aside.

4. In a large pan melt 1 tablespoon butter and add onion. Saute until translucent and add sherry and 1 quart of seafood stock. Bring to a boil and add flour mixture, stirring constantly. Reduce heat and simmer for 10 minutes. Add half and half and paprika to color.

5. Add fish, scallops, shrimp, and lobster meat. Stir to combine.

6. Divide mixture into 6 or 8 individual oven-proof crocks, depending on size of crocks.

7. Cut puff pastry slightly larger than crocks. Cover crocks with pastry taking care that pastry doesn't rest on seafood. In a small bowl beat egg and water and brush lightly onto pastry. Bake until pastry rises and turns golden brown, approximately 20 minutes.

8. Remove from oven and serve while hot with your favorite vegetable.

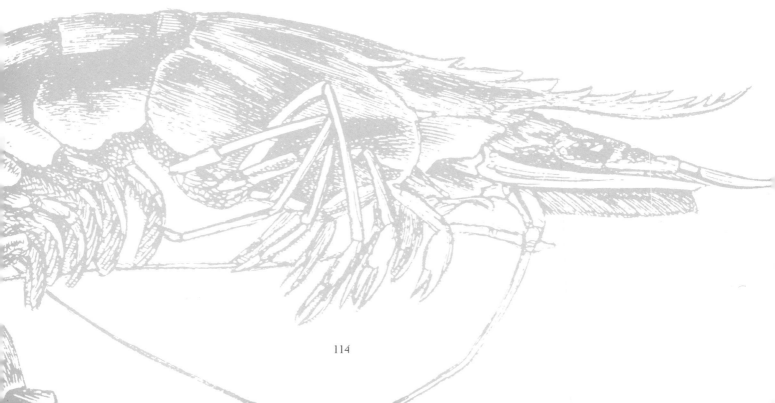

Make this tasty dish year-round for rave reviews. If you want to substitute fresh peaches, you should precook them and thicken with cornstarch in order to keep the 2 layers distinct from one another.

Peach Cobbler
Serves 8

2 29-ounce cans sliced peaches
1 cup packed brown sugar
2/3 cups pecans, chopped
1 tablespoon ground cinnamon
1-1/2 cups sugar
1-1/2 cups all-purpose flour
3 teaspoons baking powder
3 eggs
1-1/4 cups whole milk
Vanilla ice cream or whipped cream

1. Preheat oven to 350 degrees.
2. Drain peaches very well (for 2 to 3 hours), transfer to a bowl and add brown sugar, pecans, and cinnamon. Mix well and spread in 13" x 9" x 2" baking dish.
3. In a mixing bowl combine sugar, flour, and baking powder. In a separate bowl beat eggs slightly and blend in milk. Add to the flour mixture until well blended. Pour this batter over peaches.
4. Bake for 45 to 50 minutes until top is firm.
5. Serve while still warm with vanilla ice cream or fresh whipped cream.

Mail-Order Sources for Hard-to-Find Items

Supermarkets now stock many ingredients that only a short time ago were considered exotic. If you cannot find items locally, perhaps this section will be helpful for you. This is a partial listing of sources in the greater New York City area. If you are having difficulty locating items, look to your nearest city.

Bibliography for Mail Order Sourcing

New York Eats
by Ed Levine
St. Martins Press
New York

Passport's Guide to Ethnic New York
by Mark Leeds
Passport Books/NTC Publishing Group
Lincolnwood, Illinois

The New York Cookbook
by Molly O'Neill
Workman Publishing
New York

Cheeses

Cheese of All Nations
153 Chambers Street
New York, NY 10007
(212) 732-0752

Manganaro Foods
488 Ninth Avenue
New York, NY 10018
(212) 563-5331
(800) 4-SALAMI

Todaro Brothers
555 Second Avenue
New York, NY 10016
(212) 532-0633

Fresh Lobsters

Grossman's Fish Market
401 Noank Road
West Mystic, CT 06388
(203) 536-1674

Ice Cream/Sorbet Makers:

Donvier brand available through
Williams-Sonoma
P. O. Box 7456
San Francisco, CA 94120-7456
(800) 541-2233

Ice Creamer brand available directly from
Nordic Ware
Minneapolis, MN 55416
(800) 328-4310

Ice Creamer sometimes available through:
Famous Brands Housewares Factory Outlets
(A division of Lechters)
500 locations nationwide

Large Gourmet Markets

Zabar's
2245 Broadway
New York, NY 10024
(212) 496-1234

Balducci's
424 Avenue of the Americas
New York, NY 10011
(212) 673-2600

Linguica Portuguese sausage
(7 pound minimum)
Sardinha's
206 Brownell Street
Fall River, MA 02720
(508) 674-2511

Smoked Salmon
Grand Central Oyster Bar and Restaurant
Grand Central Station, Lower Level
New York, NY 10016
(212) 490-6650

Maison Glass
11 East 58th Street
New York, NY 10022
(212) 755-3316

Spices
New Orleans School of Cooking (Gumbo File)
620 Decatur Street
New Orleans, LA 70130
(800) 237-4841

The Spice Hunter (Jerk Seasoning)
254 Granada Drive
San Luis Obispo, CA 93401
(800) 444-3061
FAX (800) 444-3096

Wild Mushrooms
Aux Delices Des Bois
4 Leonard Street
New York, NY 10013
(212) 334-1230

Grace's Marketplace
1237 Third Avenue
New York, NY 10021
(212) 737-0600

To order additional copies of Sailing Through Dinner: Call or fax 203-535-1151 or mail your order to Three Squares Press, 17 Oak Street, Lords Point, Stonington, CT 06378 Your friends and family will welcome such a thoughtful gift.

Please send me _____ copies of Sailing Through Dinner @ $9.95 $ _____

Add 6% CT sales tax if books are to be shipped within CT   _____

Shipping charge for up to 2 books   3.50

Add $1.00 for each additional book shipped   _____

Total: $ _____

Name _____

Address _____

_____

Method of Payment: ___ Check Enclosed (made payable to Three Squares Press) Or
___ MasterCard/Visa ___ __ __ __ - __ __ __ __ - __ __ __ __ - __ __ __ __

Exp. Date ____ / ____   Signature_____

Index

SAILING THROUGH DINNER Special Offer Coupon
$5.00 off When Purchasing Dinner for Two (Valid 10/1 - 5/1)
Boatyard Cafe at Dodson's Boatyard
194 Water Street, Stonington, CT 06378 • 203-535-1381
Cannot Be Used in Conjunction with Other Discount Coupons.

SAILING THROUGH DINNER Special Offer Coupon
Free Bottle of House Wine When Purchasing Dinner for Two
Captain Daniel Packer Inne
32 Water Street, Mystic, CT 06355 • 203-536-3555
Cannot Be Used in Conjunction with Other Discount Coupons. (Must be of Legal CT Drinking Age.)

SAILING THROUGH DINNER Special Offer Coupon
Complimentary Glass of House Wine with Each Entree Purchased
Flood Tide Restaurant at The Inn at Mystic
Junction Routes 1 & 27, Mystic, CT 06355 • 203-536-8140
Cannot Be Used in Conjunction with Other Discount Coupons. (Must be of Legal CT Drinking Age.)

SAILING THROUGH DINNER Special Offer Coupon
One Free Dessert when Purchasing Dinner for Two
J. P. Daniels
Route 184, Gold Star Highway, Old Mystic, CT 06372 • 203-572-9564
Cannot Be Used in Conjunction with Other Discount Coupons.

SAILING THROUGH DINNER Special Offer Coupon
Free Dinner Entree with Purchase of Additional Entree
(Lower-priced entree is free.) No limit to the size of party. Expires 12/31/94
The Mooring at the Mystic Hilton
20 Coogan Boulevard, Mystic, CT 06355 • 203-572-0731
Cannot Be Used in Conjunction with Other Discount Coupons or on Holidays.

SAILING THROUGH DINNER Special Offer Coupon
10% Discount on Food Purchases Only (Valid 9/15 - 3/15)
One South Cafe
201 North Main Street, Stonington, CT 06378 • 203-536-0418
Cannot Be Used in Conjunction with Other Discount Coupons.

SAILING THROUGH DINNER Special Offer Coupon
$5.00 Off When Purchasing Dinner for Two (Valid 11/1 - 4/1)
S. & P. Oyster Company
1 Holmes Street, Mystic, CT 06355 • 203-536-2674
Cannot Be Used in Conjunction with Other Discount Coupons.

SAILING THROUGH DINNER Special Offer Coupon
Complimentary Glass of House Wine with Each Entree Purchased
Seahorse Restaurant
65 Marsh Road, Noank, CT 06340 • 203-536-1670
Cannot Be Used in Conjunction with Other Discount Coupons. (Must be of CT Legal Drinking Age.)

SAILING THROUGH DINNER Special Offer Coupon
Complimentary Glass of House Wine
or Dessert with Each Entree Purchased
Seamen's Inne Restaurant
105 Greenmanville Avenue (Route 27), Mystic, CT 06355 • 203-536-9649
Cannot Be Used in Conjunction with Other Discount Coupons. (Must be of CT Legal Drinking Age.)

SAILING THROUGH DINNER Special Offer Coupon
$2.00 Off Each Pound of Large Shrimp Purchased or
$1.00 Off Each Pound of Swordfish Purchased
Grossman's Fish Market
401 Noank Road, West Mystic, CT 06388 • 203-536-1674
Cannot Be Used in Conjunction with Other Discount Coupons.

Thank you for patronizing all of the restaurants, retail establishments and printing industry firms who participated so willingly in this fund-raising publication.